Next Generation Accuplacer Math Study Guide

To obtain permission(s) to use the material from this work for any purpose including workshops or seminars, please submit a written request to

Smart Edition Media
36 Gorham Street
Suite 1
Cambridge, MA 02138

Email: info@smarteditionmedia.com

Library of Congress Cataloging-in-Publication Data
Smart Edition Media.
Next Generation Accuplacer Math: Full Study Guide and Test Strategies for the Next Generation Accuplacer Math Exam /Smart Edition Media.

ISBN: 978-1-949147-17-9, 1st edition

1. Next Generation Accuplacer Math
2. Study Guides
3. Accuplacer Math
4. College Preparation
5. Careers

Disclaimer:

Printed in the United States of America

Next Generation Accuplacer Math: Full Study Guide and Test Strategies for the Next Generation Accuplacer Math Exam /Smart Edition Media.

ISBN: 978-1-949147-17-9 (Paperback)
        978-1-949147-04-9 (Ebook)

Print and Ebook Composition by Book Genesis, Inc. (info@bookgenesis.com)

ACCUPLACER MATH PRACTICE ONLINE

Smart Edition Media's Online Learning Resources allow you the flexibility to study for your exam on your own schedule and are the perfect companion to help you reach your goals! You can access online content with an Internet connection from any computer, laptop, or mobile device.

Online Learning Resources

Designed to enable you to master the content in quick bursts of focused learning, these tools cover a complete range of subjects, including:

- English Language Arts
- Reading
- Math
- Science
- Writing

Our online resources are filled with test-taking tips and strategies, important facts, and practice problems that mirror questions on the exam.

Online Sample Tests & Flashcards

Access additional full-length practice tests online!

Use these tests as a diagnostic tool to determine areas of strength and weakness before embarking on your study program or to assess mastery of skills once you have completed your studies.

FLASHCARDS **GAMES** **QUIZZES** **TESTS**

Go to the URL: **https://smarteditionmedia.com/pages/ accuplacermath-online-resources** and follow the password/login instructions.

TABLE OF CONTENTS

Introduction

Next Generation Accuplacer Overview

The Next Generation Accuplacer is a standardized exam that is published by the College Board. It is used as part of an overall assessment of qualifications to assess an individual's preparedness for postsecondary education.

Accuplacer is a computer-based, computer-adaptive assessment exam that is designed to determine a student's academic skills in reading, writing, and math. The exam consists of five tests containing multiple-choice questions that are administered without time limits. There are no passing or failing grades for the Accuplacer. Academic skill is identified based on how well students perform on the test. Colleges will determine whether or not students have the appropriate academic skill for admission based on how they perform.

The ACCUPLACER exam has been used by high schools, community colleges, four-year colleges, and technical schools for over 30 years; it is dedicated to supporting students with a variety of backgrounds and goals. The ACCUPLACER is an ideal exam for students hoping to enter traditional two-year colleges and career/technical schools. In addition, ACCUPLACER offers English as a Second Language (ESL) in reading, language usage, listening, and writing to support future college placement for ESL students.

An additional use of the ACCUPLACER is for academic advisors working with high school students. ACCUPLACER can help advisors determine if a student will be ready for college-level courses, or if they might benefit from taking transitional/developmental courses before enrolling into their program of choice.

Be sure to contact your school of choice to determine if ACCUPLACER is accepted.

About This Book

This book provides you with three accurate and complete representations of the mathematics sections of the ACCUPLACER standardized exam. These sections are: (1) Arithmetic; (2) Qualitative Reasoning, Algebra and Statistics; and (3) Advanced Algebra and Functions.

The reviews in this book are designed to provide the information and strategies you need to do well on the math sections of the exam. The math section practice tests in the book are based on the ACCUPLACER and contain questions similar to those you can expect to encounter on the official test. A detailed answer key follows each practice quiz and test. These answer keys provide explanations designed to help you completely understand the test material. Each explanation references the book chapter to allow you to go back to that section for additional review, if necessary.

ONLINE SAMPLE TESTS

The purchase of this book grants you access to an additional full-length math practice test online. You can locate this exams on the Smart Edition Media website.

Go to the URL: https://smarteditionmedia.com/pages/accuplacermath-online-resources and follow the password/login instructions.

ACCUPLACER BASICS

Test dates
- Contact the school which you will be attending for test dates and locations

How to register for the ACCUPLACER
- Create an account
- Follow prompts to register and pay for test

Price
- ~$15-$50
- Cost will be determined by school administering the test

How long is the test?
- There is no time limit
- Generally takes about 45-90 minutes to complete

What subjects are on the test?
- Reading, Writing, Math

How many questions are on the test?
- Each section test contains 20 questions

Where do I take the test?
- At the college where you will be enrolled
- Contact your school about test dates and locations

How long does it take to get the test score?
- Score reports are available immediately upon finishing the exam.

What to bring/not bring to the test?
- Bring:

  - Valid, government issued ID
  - Know or bring Social Security number
  - Receipt of payment for the test

- Do Not Bring

  - Calculator, one will be provided to you for use on *some* questions

How to Use This Book

Studies show that most people begin preparing for college-entry exams approximately 8 weeks before their test date. If you are scheduled to take your test in sooner than 8 weeks, do not despair! Smart Edition Media has designed this study guide to be flexible to allow you to concentrate on areas where you need the most support.

Whether you have 8 weeks to study—or much less than that—we urge you to take advantage of our online diagnostic tests to determine areas of strength and weakness, if you have not done so already. The diagnostic tests are arranged by subject area and can be found online at www.smarteditionmedia.com.

Once you have completed the online diagnostic tests, use this information to help you create a study plan that suits your individual study habits and time frame. If you are short on time, look at your diagnostic test results to determine which subject matter could use the most attention and focus the majority of your efforts on those areas. While this study guide is organized to follow the order of the actual test, you are not required to complete the book from beginning to end, in that exact order.

How This Book Is Organized

Take a look at the Table of Contents. Notice that each **Section** in the study guide corresponds to a subtest of the exam. These sections are broken into **Chapters** that identify the major content categories of the exam.

Each chapter is further divided into individual **Lessons** that address the specific content and objectives required to pass the exam. Some lessons contain embedded example questions to assess your comprehension of the content "in the moment." All lessons contain a bulleted list called "**Let's Review.**" Use this list to refresh your memory before taking a practice quiz, test, or the actual exam. A **Practice Quiz**, designed to check your progress as you move through the content, follows each chapter.

Whether you plan on working through the study guide from cover to cover, or selecting specific sections to review, each chapter of this book can be completed in one sitting. If you must end your study session before finishing a chapter, try to complete your current lesson in order to maximize comprehension and retention of the material.

Study Strategies and Tips

MAKE STUDY SESSIONS A PRIORITY.

- Use a calendar to schedule your study sessions. Set aside a dedicated amount of time each day/week for studying. While it may seem difficult to manage, given your other responsibilities, remember that in order to reach your goals, it is crucial to dedicate the time now to prepare for this test. A satisfactory score on your exam is the key to unlocking a multitude of opportunities for your future success.

- Do you work? Have children? Other obligations? Be sure to take these into account when creating your schedule. Work around them to ensure that your scheduled study sessions can be free of distractions.

TIPS FOR FINDING TIME TO STUDY.

Wake up 1-2 hours before your family for some quiet time

Study 1-2 hours before bedtime and after everything has quieted down

Utilize weekends for longer study periods

Hire a babysitter to watch children

TAKE PRACTICE TESTS

- Smart Edition Media offers practice tests, both online and in print. Take as many as you can to help be prepared. This will eliminate any surprises you may encounter during the exam.

KNOW YOUR LEARNING STYLE

- Identify your strengths and weaknesses as a student. All students are different and everyone has a different learning style. Do not compare yourself to others.
- Howard Gardner, a developmental psychologist at Harvard University, has studied the ways in which people learn new information. He has identified seven distinct intelligences. According to his theory:

"we are all able to know the world through language, logical-mathematical analysis, spatial representation, musical thinking, the use of the body to solve problems or to make things, an understanding of other individuals, and an understanding of ourselves. Where individuals differ is in the strength of these intelligences—the so-called profile of intelligences—and in the ways in which such intelligences are invoked and combined to carry out different tasks, solve diverse problems, and progress in various domains."

- Knowing your learning style can help you to tailor your studying efforts to suit your natural strengths.
- What ways help you learn best? Videos? Reading textbooks? Find the best way for you to study and learn/review the material

WHAT IS YOUR LEARNING STYLE?

Visual-Spatial – Do you like to draw, do jigsaw puzzles, read maps, daydream? Creating drawings, graphic organizers, or watching videos might be useful for you.

Bodily-Kinesthetic – Do you like movement, making things, physical activity? Do you communicate well through body language, or like to be taught through physical activity? Hands-on learning, acting out, role playing are tools you might try.

Musical – Do you show sensitivity to rhythm and sound? If you love music, and are also sensitive to sounds in your environments, it might be beneficial to study with music in the background. You can turn lessons into lyrics or speak rhythmically to aid in content retention.

Interpersonal – Do you have many friends, empathy for others, street smarts, and interact well with others? You might learn best in a group setting. Form a study group with other students who are preparing for the same exam. Technology makes it easy to connect, if you are unable to meet in person, teleconferencing or video chats are useful tools to aid interpersonal learners in connecting with others.

Intrapersonal – Do you prefer to work alone rather than in a group? Are you in tune with your inner feelings, follow your intuition and possess a strong will, confidence and opinions? Independent study and introspection will be ideal for you. Reading books, using creative materials, keeping a diary of your progress will be helpful. Intrapersonal learners are the most independent of the learners.

Linguistic – Do you use words effectively, have highly developed auditory skills and often think in words? Do you like reading, playing word games, making up poetry or stories? Learning tools such as computers, games, multimedia will be beneficial to your studies.

Logical-Mathematical – Do you think conceptually, abstractly, and are able to see and explore patterns and relationships? Try exploring subject matter through logic games, experiments and puzzles.

CREATE THE OPTIMAL STUDY ENVIRONMENT

- Some people enjoy listening to soft background music when they study. (Instrumental music is a good choice.) Others need to have a silent space in order to concentrate. Which do you prefer? Either way, it is best to create an environment that is free of distractions for your study sessions.

- Have study guide – Will travel! Leave your house: Daily routines and chores can be distractions. Check out your local library, a coffee shop, or other quiet space to remove yourself from distractions and daunting household tasks will compete for your attention.

- Create a Technology Free Zone. Silence the ringer on your cell phone and place it out of reach to prevent surfing the Web, social media interactions, and email/texting exchanges. Turn off the television, radio, or other devices while you study.

- Are you comfy? Find a comfortable, but not *too* comfortable, place to study. Sit at a desk or table in a straight, upright chair. Avoid sitting on the couch, a bed, or in front of the TV. Wear clothing that is not binding and restricting.

- Keep your area organized. Have all the materials you need available and ready: Smart Edition study guide, computer, notebook, pen, calculator, and pencil/eraser. Use a desk lamp or overhead light that provides ample lighting to prevent eye-strain and fatigue.

HEALTHY BODY, HEALTHY MIND

- Consider these words of wisdom from Buddha, "To keep the body in good health is a duty—otherwise we shall not be able to keep our mind strong and clear."

KEYS TO CREATING A HEALTHY BODY AND MIND:

Drink water – Stay hydrated! Limit drinks with excessive sugar or caffeine.

Eat natural foods – Make smart food choices and avoid greasy, fatty, sugary foods.

Think positively – You can do this! Do not doubt yourself, and trust in the process.

Exercise daily – If you have a workout routine, stick to it! If you are more sedentary, now is a great time to begin! Try yoga or a low-impact sport. Simply walking at a brisk pace will help to get your heart rate going.

Sleep well – Getting a good night's sleep is important, but too few of us actually make it a priority. Aim to get eight hours of uninterrupted sleep in order to maximize your mental focus, memory, learning, and physical wellbeing.

FINAL THOUGHTS

- Remember to relax and take breaks during study sessions.
- Review the testing material. Go over topics you already know for a refresher.
- Focus more time on less familiar subjects.

EXAM PREPARATION

In addition to studying for your upcoming exam, it is important to keep in mind that you need to prepare your mind and body as well. When preparing to take an exam as a whole, not just studying, taking practice exams, and reviewing math rules, it is critical to prepare your body in order to be mentally and physically ready. Often, your success rate will be much higher when you are *fully* ready.

Here are some tips to keep in mind when preparing for your exam:

SEVERAL WEEKS/DAYS BEFORE THE EXAM

- Get a full night of sleep, approximately 8 hours
- Turn off electronics before bed
- Exercise regularly
- Eat a healthy balanced diet, include fruits and vegetable
- Drink water

THE NIGHT BEFORE

- Eat a good dinner
- Pack materials/bag, healthy snacks, and water

- Gather materials needed for test: your ID and receipt of test. You do not want to be scrambling the morning of the exam. If you are unsure of what to bring with you, check with your testing center or test administrator.
- Map the location of test center, identify how you will be getting there (driving, public transportation, uber, etc.), when you need to leave, and parking options.
- Lay your clothes out. Wear comfortable clothes and shoes, do not wear items that are too hot/cold
- Allow minimum of ~8 hours of sleep
- Avoid coffee and alcohol
- Do not take any medications or drugs to help you sleep
- Set alarm

THE DAY OF THE EXAM

- Wake up early, allow ample time to do all the things you need to do and for travel
- Eat a healthy, well-rounded breakfast
- Drink water
- Leave early and arrive early, leave time for any traffic or any other unforeseeable circumstances
- Arrive early and check in for exam. This will give you enough time to relax, take off coat, and become comfortable with your surroundings.

Take a deep breath, get ready, go! You got this!

SECTION I
ARITHMETIC

Chapter 1 Numbers and Basic Operations

Basic Addition and Subtraction

This lesson introduces the concept of numbers and their symbolic and graphical representations. It also describes how to add and subtract whole numbers.

Numbers

A **number** is a way to quantify a set of entities that share some characteristic. For example, a fruit basket might contain nine pieces of fruit. More specifically, it might contain three apples, two oranges, and four bananas. Note that a number is a quantity, but a **numeral** is the symbol that represents the number: 8 means the number eight, for instance.

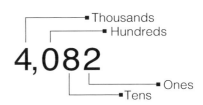

Although number representations vary, the most common is **base 10**. In base-10 format, each **digit** (or individual numeral) in a number is a quantity based on a multiple of 10. The base-10 system designates 0 through 9 as the numerals for zero through nine, respectively, and combines them to represent larger numbers. Thus, after counting from 1 to 9, the next number uses an additional digit: 10. That number means 1 group of 10 ones plus 0 additional ones. After 99, another digit is necessary, this time representing a hundred (10 sets of 10). This process of adding digits can go on indefinitely to express increasingly large numbers. For whole numbers, the rightmost digit is the ones place, the next digit to its left is the tens place, the next is the hundreds place, then the thousands place, and so on.

Classifying numbers can be convenient. The chart below lists a few common number sets.

Sets of Numbers	Members	Remarks
Natural numbers	1, 2, 3, 4, 5,...	The "counting" numbers
Whole numbers	0, 1, 2, 3, 4,...	The natural numbers plus 0
Integers	..., −3, −2, −1, 0, 1, 2, 3,...	The whole numbers plus all negative whole numbers
Real numbers	All numbers	The integers plus all fraction/decimal numbers in between
Rational numbers	All real numbers that can be expressed as p/q, where p and q are integers and q is nonzero	The natural numbers, whole numbers, and integers are all rational numbers
Irrational numbers	All real numbers that are not rational	The rational and irrational numbers together constitute the entire set of real numbers

Example

Jane has 4 pennies, 3 dimes, and 7 dollars. How many cents does she have?

A. 347   B. 437   C. 734   D. 743

The correct answer is **C**. The correct solution is 734. A penny is 1 cent. A dime (10 pennies) is 10 cents, and a dollar (100 pennies) is 100 cents. Place the digits in base-10 format: 7 hundreds, 3 tens, 4 ones, or 734.

The Number Line

The **number line** is a model that illustrates the relationships among numbers. The complete number line is infinite and includes every real number—both positive and negative. A ruler, for example, is a portion of a number line that assigns a **unit** (such as inches or centimeters) to each number. Typically, number lines depict smaller numbers to the left and larger numbers to the right. For example, a portion of the number line centered on 0 might look like the following:

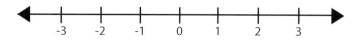

Because people learn about numbers in part through counting, they have a basic sense of how to order them. The number line builds on this sense by placing all the numbers (at least conceptually) from least to greatest. Whether a particular number is greater than or less than another is determined by comparing their relative positions. One number is greater than another if it is farther right on the number line. Likewise, a number is less than another if it is farther left on the number line. Symbolically, < means "is less than" and > means "is greater than." For example, $5 > 1$ and $9 < 25$.

Example

Place the following numbers in order from greatest to least: 5, –12, 0.

A. 0, 5, –12   C. 5, 0, –12

B. –12, 5, 0   D. –12, 0, 5

> **BE CAREFUL!**
>
> When ordering negative numbers, think of the number line. Although $-10 > -2$ may seem correct, it is incorrect. Because -10 is to the left of -2 on the number line, $-10 < -2$.

The correct answer is **C**. The correct solution is 5, 0, –12. Use the number line to order the numbers. Note that the question says *from greatest to least.*

Addition

Addition is the process of combining two or more numbers. For example, one set has 4 members and another set has 5 members. To combine the sets and find out how many members are in the new set, add 4 and 5 to get the **sum.** Symbolically, the expression is $4 + 5$, where + is the **plus sign.** Pictorially, it might look like the following:

To get the sum, combine the two sets of circles and then count them. The result is 9.

> **KEY POINT**
> The order of the numbers is irrelevant when adding.

Another way to look at addition involves the number line. When adding 4 + 5, for example, start at 4 on the number line and take 5 steps to the right. The stopping point will be 9, which is the sum.

Counting little pictures or using the number line works for small numbers, but it becomes unwieldy for large ones—even numbers such as 24 and 37 would be difficult to add quickly and accurately. A simple algorithm enables much faster addition of large numbers. It works with two or more numbers.

STEP BY STEP

Step 1. Stack the numbers, vertically aligning the digits for each place.

Step 2. Draw a plus sign (+) to the left of the bottom number and draw a horizontal line below the last number.

Step 3. Add the digits in the ones place.

Step 4. If the sum from Step 3 is less than 10, write it in the same column below the horizontal line. Otherwise, write the first (ones) digit below the line, then **carry** the second (tens) digit to the top of the next column.

Step 5. Going from right to left, repeat Steps 3–4 for the other places.

Step 6. If applicable, write the remaining carry digit as the leftmost digit in the sum.

Example

Evaluate the expression 154 + 98.

A. 250   B. 252   C. 352   D. 15,498

The correct answer is **B**. The correct solution is 252. Carefully follow the addition algorithm (see below). The process involves carrying a digit twice.

$$
\begin{array}{r} 154 \\ + 98 \\ \hline \end{array} \rightarrow
\begin{array}{r} {\scriptstyle 1} \\ 154 \\ + 98 \\ \hline 2 \end{array} \rightarrow
\begin{array}{r} {\scriptstyle 1\,1} \\ 154 \\ + 98 \\ \hline 52 \end{array} \rightarrow
\begin{array}{r} {\scriptstyle 1\,1} \\ 154 \\ + 98 \\ \hline 252 \end{array}
$$

Subtraction

Subtraction is the inverse (opposite) of addition. Instead of representing the sum of numbers, it represents the difference between them. For example, given a set containing 15 members, subtracting 3 of those members yields a **difference** of 12. Using the **minus sign**, the expression for this operation is 15 − 3 = 12. As with addition, two approaches are counting pictures and using the number line. The first case might involve drawing 15 circles and then crossing off 3 of them; the difference is the number of remaining circles (12). To use the number line, begin at 15 and move left 3 steps to reach 12.

Again, these approaches are unwieldy for large numbers, but the subtraction algorithm eases evaluation by hand. This algorithm is only practical for two numbers at a time.

STEP BY STEP

Step 1. Stack the numbers, vertically aligning the digits in each place. Put the number you are subtracting *from* on top.

Step 2. Draw a minus sign (−) to the left of the bottom number and draw a horizontal line below the stack of numbers.

Step 3. Start at the ones place. If the digit at the top is larger than the digit below it, write the difference under the line. Otherwise, **borrow** from the top digit in the next-higher place by crossing it off, subtracting 1 from it, and writing the difference above it. Then add 10 to the digit in the ones place and perform the subtraction as normal.

Step 4. Going from right to left, repeat Step 3 for the rest of the places. If borrowing was necessary, make sure to use the new digit in each place, not the original one.

When adding or subtracting with negative numbers, the following rules are helpful. Note that x and y are used as placeholders for any real number.

$x + (-y) = x - y$

$-x - y = -(x + y)$

$(-x) + (-y) = -(x + y)$

$x - y = -(y - x)$

BE CAREFUL!

When dealing with numbers that have units (such as weights, currencies, or volumes), addition and subtraction are only possible when the numbers have the same unit. If necessary, convert one or more of them to equivalent numbers with the same unit.

Example

Kevin has 120 minutes to complete an exam. If he has already used 43, how many minutes does he have left?

   A. 43   B. 77   C. 87   D. 163

The correct answer is **B**. The correct solution is 77. The first step is to convert this problem to a math expression. The goal is to find the difference between how many minutes Kevin has for the exam and how many he has left after 43 minutes have elapsed. The expression would be 120 – 43. Carefully follow the subtraction algorithm (see below). The process will involve borrowing a digit twice.

$$
\begin{array}{c}
120 \\
-\ 43 \\
\hline
\end{array}
\longrightarrow
\begin{array}{c}
\overset{1\ 10}{1\cancel{2}0} \\
-\ 43 \\
\hline
7
\end{array}
\longrightarrow
\begin{array}{c}
\overset{0\ 11 10}{\cancel{1}\cancel{2}0} \\
-\ 43 \\
\hline
77
\end{array}
$$

Let's Review!

- Numbers are positive and negative quantities and often appear in base-10 format.
- The number line illustrates the ordering of numbers.
- Addition is the combination of numbers. It can be performed by counting objects or pictures, moving on the number line, or using the addition algorithm.
- Subtraction is finding the difference between numbers. Like addition, it can be performed by counting, moving on the number line, or using the subtraction algorithm.

BASIC MULTIPLICATION AND DIVISION

This lesson describes the process of multiplying and dividing numbers and introduces the order of operations, which governs how to evaluate expressions containing multiple arithmetic operations.

Multiplication

Addition can be tedious if it involves multiple instances of the same numbers. For example, evaluating 29 + 29 is easy, but evaluating 29 + 29 + 29 + 29 + 29 is laborious. Note that this example contains five instances—or multiples—of 29. **Multiplication** replaces the repeated addition of the same number with a single, more concise operation. Using the **multiplication (or times) symbol** (×), the expression is

$$29 + 29 + 29 + 29 + 29 = 5 \times 29$$

The expression contains 5 multiples of 29. These numbers are the **factors** of multiplication. The result is called the **product**. In this case, addition shows that the product is 145. As with the other arithmetic operations, multiplication is easy for small numbers. Below is the multiplication table for whole numbers up to 12.

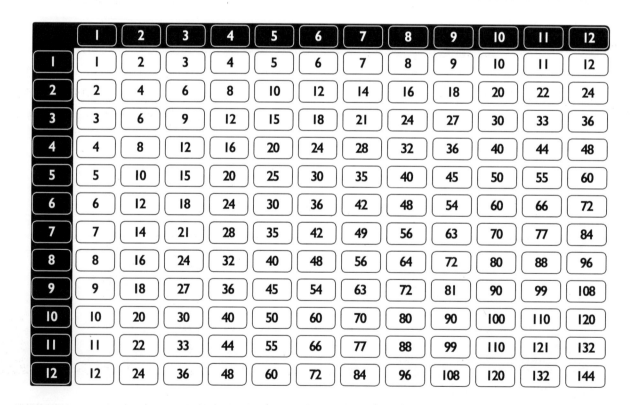

When dealing with large numbers, the multiplication algorithm is more practical than memorization. The ability to quickly recall the products in the multiplication table is nevertheless crucial to using this algorithm.

STEP BY STEP

Step 1. Stack the two factors, vertically aligning the digits in each place.

Step 2. Draw a multiplication symbol (×) to the left of the bottom number and draw a horizontal line below the stack.

Step 3. Begin with the ones digit in the lower factor. Multiply it with the ones digit from the top factor.

Step 4. If the product from Step 3 is less than 10, write it in the same column below the horizontal line. Otherwise, write the first (ones) digit below the line and carry the second (tens) digit to the top of the next column.

Step 5. Perform Step 4 for each digit in the top factor, adding any carry digit to the result. If an extra carry digit appears at the end, write it as the leftmost digit in the product.

Step 6. Going right to left, repeat Steps 3–4 for the other places in the bottom factor, starting a new line in each case.

Step 7. Add the numbers below the line to get the product.

Example

A certain type of screw comes in packs of 35. If a contractor orders 52 packs, how many screws does he receive?

   A. 2   B. 57   C. 245   D. 1,820

The correct answer is **D**. The first step is to convert this problem to a math expression. The goal is to find how many screws the contractor receives if he orders 52 packs of 35 each. The expression would be 52 × 35 (or 35 × 52). Carefully follow the multiplication algorithm (see below).

$$
\begin{array}{r} 52 \\ \times\ 35 \\ \hline \end{array}
\rightarrow
\begin{array}{r} {\scriptstyle 1} \\ 52 \\ \times\ 35 \\ \hline 0 \end{array}
\rightarrow
\begin{array}{r} {\scriptstyle 1} \\ 52 \\ \times\ 35 \\ \hline 260 \end{array}
\rightarrow
\begin{array}{r} {\scriptstyle 1} \\ 52 \\ \times\ 35 \\ \hline 260 \\ 6 \end{array}
\rightarrow
\begin{array}{r} {\scriptstyle 1\ 1} \\ 52 \\ \times\ 35 \\ \hline 260 \\ 56 \end{array}
\rightarrow
\begin{array}{r} {\scriptstyle 1\ 1} \\ 52 \\ \times\ 35 \\ \hline 260 \\ 156 \end{array}
\rightarrow
\begin{array}{r} {\scriptstyle 1\ 1} \\ 52 \\ \times\ 35 \\ \hline 260 \\ +\ 156 \\ \hline 1{,}820 \end{array}
$$

KEY POINT

As with addition, the order of numbers in a multiplication expression is irrelevant to the product. For example, 6 × 9 = 9 × 6.

Division

Division is the inverse of multiplication, like subtraction is the inverse of addition. Whereas multiplication asks how many individuals are in 8 groups of 9 ($8 \times 9 = 72$), for example, division asks how many groups of 8 (or 9) are in 72. Division expressions use either the / or ÷ symbol. Therefore, $72 \div 9$ means: How many groups of 9 are in 72, or how many times does 9 go into 72? Thinking about the meaning of multiplication shows that $72 \div 9 = 8$ and $72 \div 8 = 9$. In the expression $72 \div 8 = 9$, 72 is the **dividend**, 8 is the **divisor**, and 9 is the **quotient.**

When the dividend is unevenly divisible by the divisor (e.g., $5 \div 2$), calculating the quotient with a **remainder** can be convenient. The quotient in this case is the maximum number of times the divisor goes into the dividend plus how much of the dividend is left over. To express the remainder, use an R. For example, the quotient of $5 \div 2$ is 2R1 because 2 goes into 5 twice with 1 left over.

Knowing the multiplication table allows quick evaluation of simple whole-number division. For larger numbers, the division algorithm enables evaluation by hand.

Unlike multiplication—but like subtraction—the order of the numbers in a division expression is important. Generally, changing the order changes the quotient.

STEP BY STEP

Step 1. Write the divisor and then the dividend on a single line.

Step 2. Draw a vertical line between them, connecting to a horizontal line over the dividend.

Step 3. If the divisor is smaller than the leftmost digit of the dividend, perform the remainder division and write the quotient (without the remainder) above that digit. If the divisor is larger than the leftmost digit, use the first two digits (or however many are necessary) until the number is greater than the divisor. Write the quotient over the rightmost digit in that number.

Step 4. Multiply the quotient digit by the divisor and write it under the dividend, vertically aligning the ones digit of the product with the quotient digit.

Step 5. Subtract the product from the digits above it.

Step 6. Bring down the next digit from the quotient.

Step 7. Perform Steps 3–6, using the most recent difference as the quotient.

Step 8. Write the remainder next to the quotient.

Example

Evaluate the expression 468 ÷ 26.

 A. 18 B. 18R2 C. 494 D. 12,168

The correct answer is **A.** Carefully follow the division algorithm. In this case, the answer has no remainder.

$$26)\overline{468} \rightarrow \begin{array}{r} 1 \\ 26)\overline{468} \\ 26 \end{array} \rightarrow \begin{array}{r} 1 \\ 26)\overline{468} \\ -26 \\ \hline 20 \end{array} \rightarrow \begin{array}{r} 1 \\ 26)\overline{468} \\ -26\downarrow \\ \hline 208 \end{array} \rightarrow \begin{array}{r} 18 \\ 26)\overline{468} \\ -26\downarrow \\ \hline 208 \\ -208 \\ \hline 0 \end{array}$$

KEY POINT
Division by 0 is undefined. If it appears in an expression, something is wrong.

Signed Multiplication and Division

Multiplying and dividing signed numbers is simpler than adding and subtracting them because it only requires remembering two simple rules. First, if the two numbers have the same sign, their product or quotient is positive. Second, if they have different signs, their product or quotient is negative.

As a result, negative numbers can be multiplied or divided as if they are positive. Just keep track of the sign separately for the product or quotient. Note that negative numbers are sometimes written in parentheses to avoid the appearance of subtraction.

For Example:

$5 \times (-3) = -15$

$(-8) \times (-8) = 64$

$(-12) \div 3 = -4$

$(-100) \div (-25) = 4$

Example

Evaluate the expression $(-7) \times (-9)$.

 A. −63 B. −16 C. 16 D. 63

The correct answer is **D.** Because both factors are negative, the product will be positive. Because the product of 7 and 9 is 63, the product of −7 and −9 is also 63.

Order of Operations

By default, math expressions work like most Western languages: they should be read and evaluated from left to right. However, some operations take precedence over others, which can change this default evaluation. Following this **order of operations** is critical. The mnemonic **PEMDAS** (**P**lease **E**xcuse **M**y **D**ear **A**unt **S**ally) helps in remembering how to evaluate an expression with multiple operations.

STEP BY STEP

P. Evaluate operations in parentheses (or braces/brackets). If the expression has parentheses within parentheses, begin with the innermost ones.

E. Evaluate exponential operations. (For expressions without exponents, ignore this step.)

MD. Perform all multiplication and division operations, going through the expression from left to right.

AS. Perform all addition and subtraction operations, going through the expression from left to right.

BE CAREFUL!

When evaluating an expression like $4 - 3 + 2 \times 5$, remember to go from left to right when adding and subtracting or when multiplying and dividing. The first step in this case (MD) yields $4 - 3 + 10$. Avoid the temptation to add first in the next step; instead, go from left to right. The result is $1 + 10 = 11$, *not* $4 - 13 = -9$.

Because the order of numbers in multiplication and addition does not affect the result, the PEMDAS procedure only requires going from left to right when dividing or subtracting. At those points, going in the correct direction is critical to getting the right answer.

Calculators that can handle a series of numbers at once automatically evaluate an expression according to the order of operations. When available, calculators are a good way to check the results.

Example

Evaluate the expression 8 × (3 + 6) ÷ 3–2 + 5.

   A. 13   B. 17   C. 27   D. 77

The correct answer is **C**. Use the PEMDAS mnemonic. Start with parentheses. Then, do multiplication/division from left to right. Finally, do addition/subtraction from left to right.

$8 \times (3 + 6) \div 3\text{–}2 + 5$

$8 \times 9 \div 3\text{–}2 + 5$

$72 \div 3\text{–}2 + 5$

$24\text{–}2 + 5$

$22 + 5$

27

Let's Review!

- The multiplication table is important to memorize for both multiplying and dividing small whole numbers (up to about 12).
- Multiplication and division of large numbers by hand typically requires the multiplication and division algorithms.
- Multiplying and dividing signed numbers follows two simple rules: If the numbers have the same sign, the product or quotient is positive. If they have different signs, the product or quotient is negative.
- When evaluating expressions with several operations, carefully follow the order of operations; PEMDAS is a helpful mnemonic.

DECIMALS AND FRACTIONS

This lesson introduces the basics of decimals and fractions. It also demonstrates changing decimals to fractions, changing fractions to decimals, and converting between fractions, decimals, and percentages.

Introduction to Fractions

A fraction represents part of a whole number. The top number of a fraction is the **numerator**, and the bottom number of a fraction is the **denominator**. The numerator is smaller than the denominator for a **proper fraction**. The numerator is larger than the denominator for an **improper fraction**.

Proper Fractions	Improper Fractions
$\frac{2}{5}$	$\frac{5}{2}$
$\frac{7}{12}$	$\frac{12}{7}$
$\frac{19}{20}$	$\frac{20}{19}$

An improper fraction can be changed to a **mixed number**. A mixed number is a whole number and a proper fraction. To write an improper fraction as a mixed number, divide the denominator into the numerator. The result is the whole number.

KEEP IN MIND

When comparing fractions, the denominators of the fractions must be the same.

The remainder is the numerator of the proper fraction, and the value of the denominator does not change. For example, $\frac{5}{2}$ is $2\frac{1}{2}$ because 2 goes into 5 twice with a remainder of 1. To write an improper fraction as a mixed number, multiply the whole number by the denominator and add the result to the numerator. The results become the new numerator. For example, $2\frac{1}{2}$ is $\frac{5}{2}$ because 2 times 2 plus 1 is 5 for the new numerator.

When comparing fractions, the denominators must be the same. Then, look at the numerator to determine which fraction is larger. If the fractions have different denominators, then a **least common denominator** must be found. This number is the smallest number that can be divided evenly into the denominators of all fractions being compared.

To determine the largest fraction from the group $\frac{1}{3}, \frac{3}{5}, \frac{2}{3}, \frac{2}{5}$, the first step is to find a common denominator. In this case, the least common denominator is 15 because 3 times 5 and 5 times 3 is 15. The second step is to convert the fractions to a denominator of 15. The fractions with a denominator of 3 have the numerator and denominator multiplied by 5, and the fractions with a denominator of 5 have the numerator and denominator multiplied by 3, as shown below:

$$\frac{1}{3} \times \frac{5}{5} = \frac{5}{15}, \frac{3}{5} \times \frac{3}{3} = \frac{9}{15}, \frac{2}{3} \times \frac{5}{5} = \frac{10}{15}, \frac{2}{5} \times \frac{3}{3} = \frac{6}{15}$$

Now, the numerators can be compared. The largest fraction is $\frac{2}{3}$ because it has a numerator of 10 after finding the common denominator.

Examples

1. **Which fraction is the least?**

   A. $\frac{3}{5}$　　　　　　B. $\frac{3}{4}$　　　　　　C. $\frac{1}{5}$　　　　　　D. $\frac{1}{4}$

   The correct answer is **C**. The correct solution is $\frac{1}{5}$ because it has the smallest numerator compared to the other fractions with the same denominator. The fractions with a common denominator of 20 are $\frac{3}{5} = \frac{12}{20}, \frac{3}{4} = \frac{15}{20}, \frac{1}{5} = \frac{4}{20}, \frac{1}{4} = \frac{5}{20}$.

2. **Which fraction is the greatest?**

   A. $\frac{5}{6}$　　　　　　B. $\frac{1}{2}$　　　　　　C. $\frac{2}{3}$　　　　　　D. $\frac{1}{6}$

   The correct answer is **A**. The correct solution is $\frac{5}{6}$ because it has the largest numerator compared to the other fractions with the same denominator. The fractions with a common denominator of 6 are $\frac{5}{6} = \frac{5}{6}, \frac{1}{2} = \frac{3}{6}, \frac{2}{3} = \frac{4}{6}, \frac{1}{6} = \frac{1}{6}$.

Introduction to Decimals

A **decimal** is a number that expresses part of a whole. Decimals show a portion of a number after a decimal point. Each number to the left and right of the decimal point has a specific place value. Identify the place values for 645.3207.

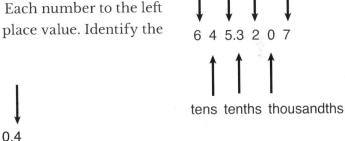

tens tenths thousandths

When comparing decimals, compare the numbers in the same place value. For example, determine the greatest decimal from the group 0.4, 0.41, 0.39, and 0.37. In these numbers, there is a value to the right of the decimal point. Comparing the tenths places, the numbers with 4 tenths (0.4 and 0.41) are greater than the numbers with three tenths (0.39 and 0.37).

0.4

0.41

KEEP IN MIND

When comparing decimals, compare the place value where the numbers are different.

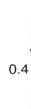

0.39

0.37

Then, compare the hundredths in the 4 tenths numbers. The value of 0.41 is greater because there is a 1 in the hundredths place versus a 0 in the hundredths place.

0.4

0.41

Here is another example: determine the least decimal of the group 5.23, 5.32, 5.13, and 5.31. In this group, the ones value is 5 for all numbers. Then, comparing the tenths values, 5.13 is the smallest number because it is the only value with 1 tenth.

5.23

5.32

5.13

5.31

Examples

1. **Which decimal is the greatest?**

   A. 0.07   B. 0.007   C. 0.7   D. 0.0007

   The correct answer is **C**. The solution is 0.7 because it has the largest place value in the tenths.

2. **Which decimal is the least?**

   A. 0.0413   B. 0.0713   C. 0.0513   D. 0.0613

   The correct answer is **A**. The correct solution is 0.0413 because it has the smallest place value in the hundredths place.

Changing Decimals and Fractions

Three steps change a decimal to a fraction.

STEP BY STEP

Step 1. Write the decimal divided by 1 with the decimal as the numerator and 1 as the denominator.

Step 2. Multiply the numerator and denominator by 10 for every number after the decimal point. (For example, if there is 1 decimal place, multiply by 10. If there are 2 decimal places, multiply by 100).

Step 3. Reduce the fraction completely.

To change the decimal 0.37 to a fraction, start by writing the decimal as a fraction with a denominator of one, $\frac{0.37}{1}$. Because there are two decimal places, multiply the numerator and denominator by 100, $\frac{0.37 \times 100}{1 \times 100} = \frac{37}{100}$. The fraction does not reduce, so $\frac{37}{100}$ is 0.37 in fraction form.

Similarly, to change the decimal 2.4 to a fraction start by writing the decimal as a fraction with a denominator of one, $\frac{0.4}{1}$, and ignore the whole number. Because there is one decimal place, multiply the numerator and denominator by 10, $\frac{0.4 \times 10}{1 \times 10} = \frac{4}{10}$. The fraction does reduce: $2\frac{4}{10} = 2\frac{2}{5}$ is 2.4 in fraction form.

The decimal $0.\overline{3}$ as a fraction is $\frac{0.\overline{3}}{1}$. In the case of a repeating decimal, let $n = 0.\overline{3}$ and $10 = 3.\overline{3}$. Then, $10n - n = 3.\overline{3} - 0.\overline{3}$, resulting in $9n = 3$ and solution of $n = \frac{3}{9} = \frac{1}{3}$. The decimal $0.\overline{3}$ is $\frac{1}{3}$ as a fraction.

Examples

1. **Change 0.38 to a fraction. Simplify completely.**

   A. $\frac{3}{10}$ B. $\frac{9}{25}$ C. $\frac{19}{50}$ D. $\frac{2}{5}$

   The correct answer is **C**. The correct solution is $\frac{19}{50}$ because $\frac{0.38}{1} = \frac{38}{100} = \frac{19}{50}$.

2. **Change $1.\overline{1}$ to a fraction. Simplify completely.**

   A. $1\frac{1}{11}$ B. $1\frac{1}{9}$ C. $1\frac{1}{6}$ D. $1\frac{1}{3}$

   The correct answer is **B**. The correct solution is $1\frac{1}{9}$. Let $n = 1.\overline{1}$ and $10n = 11.\overline{1}$. Then, $10n - n = 11.\overline{1} - 1.\overline{1}$, resulting in $9n = 10$ and solution of $n = \frac{10}{9} = 1\frac{1}{9}$.

Two steps change a fraction to a decimal.

STEP BY STEP

Step 1. Divide the denominator by the numerator. Add zeros after the decimal point as needed.

Step 2. Complete the process when there is no remainder or the decimal is repeating.

To convert $\frac{1}{5}$ to a decimal, rewrite $\frac{1}{5}$ as a long division problem and add zeros after the decimal point, $1.0 \div 5$. Complete the long division and $\frac{1}{5}$ as a decimal is 0.2. The division is complete because there is no remainder.

To convert $\frac{8}{9}$ to a decimal, rewrite $\frac{8}{9}$ as a long division problem and add zeros after the decimal point, $8.00 \div 9$. Complete the long division, and $\frac{8}{9}$ as a decimal is $0.\overline{8}$. The process is complete because the decimal is complete.

To rewrite the mixed number $2\frac{3}{4}$ as a decimal, the fraction needs changed to a decimal. Rewrite $\frac{3}{4}$ as a long division problem and add zeros after the decimal point, $3.00 \div 4$. The whole number is needed for the answer and is not included in the long division. Complete the long division, and $2\frac{3}{4}$ as a decimal is 2.75.

Examples

1. Change $\frac{9}{10}$ to a decimal. Simplify completely.

   A. 0.75   B. 0.8   C. 0.85   D. 0.9

   The correct answer is **D**. The correct answer is 0.9 because $\frac{9}{10} = 9.0 \div 10 = 0.9$.

2. Change $\frac{5}{6}$ to a decimal. Simplify completely.

   A. 0.73   B. $0.7\overline{6}$ C. $0.8\overline{3}$ D. 0.86

   The correct answer is **C**. The correct answer is $0.8\overline{3}$ because $\frac{5}{6} = 5.000 \div 6 = 0.8\overline{3}$.

Convert among Fractions, Decimals, and Percentages

Fractions, decimals, and percentages can change forms, but they are equivalent values.

There are two ways to change a decimal to a percent. One way is to multiply the decimal by 100 and add a percent sign. 0.24 as a percent is 24%.

Another way is to move the decimal point two places to the right. The decimal 0.635 is 63.5% as a percent when moving the decimal point two places to the right.

Any decimal, including repeating decimals, can change to a percent. $0.\overline{3}$ as a percent is $0.\overline{3} \times 100 = 33.\overline{3}\%$.

Example

Write 0.345 as a percent.

   A. 3.45%   B. 34.5%   C. 345%   D. 3450%

   The correct answer is **B**. The correct answer is 34.5% because 0.345 as a percent is 34.5%.

There are two ways to change a percent to a decimal. One way is to remove the percent sign and divide the decimal by 100. For example, 73% as a decimal is 0.73.

Another way is to move the decimal point two places to the left. For example, 27.8% is 0.278 as a decimal when moving the decimal point two places to the left.

Any percent, including repeating percents, can change to a decimal. For example, $44.\overline{4}\%$ as a decimal is $44.\overline{4} \div 100 = 0.\overline{4}$.

Example

Write 131% as a decimal.

   A. 0.131   B. 1.31   C. 13.1   D. 131

   The correct answer is **B**. The correct answer is 1.31 because 131% as a decimal is $131 \div 100 = 1.31$.

Decimals and Fractions

Two steps change a fraction to a percent.

> **STEP BY STEP**
> **Step 1.** Divide the numerator and denominator.
> **Step 2.** Multiply by 100 and add a percent sign.

To change the fraction $\frac{3}{5}$ to a decimal, perform long division to get 0.6. Then, multiply 0.6 by 100 and $\frac{3}{5}$ is the same as 60%.

To change the fraction $\frac{7}{8}$ to a decimal, perform long division to get 0.875. Then, multiply 0.875 by 100 and $\frac{7}{8}$ is the same as 87.5%.

Fractions that are repeating decimals can also be converted to a percent. To change the fraction $\frac{2}{3}$ to a decimal, perform long division to get $0.\overline{6}$. Then, multiply $0.\overline{6}$ by 100 and the percent is $66.\overline{6}\%$.

Example

Write $2\frac{1}{8}$ as a percent.

    A. 21.2%   B. 21.25%   C. 212%   D. 212.5%

The correct answer is **D.** The correct answer is 212.5% because $2\frac{1}{8}$ as a percent is 2.125 x 100 = 212.5%.

Two steps change a percent to a fraction.

> **STEP BY STEP**
> **Step 1.** Remove the percent sign and write the value as the numerator with a denominator of 100.
> **Step 2.** Simplify the fraction.

Remove the percent sign from 45% and write as a fraction with a denominator of 100, $\frac{45}{100}$. The fraction reduces to $\frac{9}{20}$.

Remove the percent sign from 22.8% and write as a fraction with a denominator of 100, $\frac{22.8}{100}$. The fraction reduces to $\frac{228}{1000} = \frac{57}{250}$.

Repeating percentages can change to a fraction. Remove the percent sign from $16.\overline{6}\%$ and write as a fraction with a denominator of 100, $\frac{16.\overline{6}}{100}$. The fraction simplifies to $\frac{0.1\overline{6}}{1} = \frac{1}{6}$.

19

Example

Write 72% as a fraction.

A. $\frac{27}{50}$ B. $\frac{7}{10}$ C. $\frac{18}{25}$ D. $\frac{3}{4}$

The correct answer is **C**. The correct answer is $\frac{18}{25}$ because 72% as a fraction is $\frac{72}{100} = \frac{18}{25}$.

Let's Review!

- A fraction is a number with a numerator and a denominator. A fraction can be written as a proper fraction, an improper fraction, or a mixed number. Changing fractions to a common denominator enables you to determine the least or greatest fraction in a group of fractions.
- A decimal is a number that expresses part of a whole. By comparing the same place values, you can find the least or greatest decimal in a group of decimals.
- A number can be written as a fraction, a decimal, and a percent. These are equivalent values. Numbers can be converted between fractions, decimals, and percents by following a series of steps.

MULTIPLICATION AND DIVISION OF FRACTIONS

This lesson introduces how to multiply and divide fractions.

Multiplying a Fraction by a Fraction

The multiplication of fractions does not require changing any denominators like adding and subtracting fractions do. To multiply a fraction by a fraction, multiply the numerators together and multiply the denominators together. For example, $\frac{2}{3} \times \frac{4}{5}$ is $\frac{2 \times 4}{3 \times 5}$, which is $\frac{8}{15}$.

Sometimes, the final solution reduces. For example, $\frac{3}{5} \times \frac{1}{9} = \frac{3 \times 1}{5 \times 9} = \frac{3}{45}$. The fraction $\frac{3}{45}$ reduces to $\frac{1}{15}$.

Simplifying fractions can occur before completing the multiplication. In the previous problem, the numerator of 3 can be simplified with the denominator of 9: $\frac{\overset{1}{\cancel{3}}}{5} \times \frac{1}{\underset{3}{\cancel{9}}} = \frac{1}{15}$. This method of simplifying only occurs with the multiplication of fractions.

> **KEEP IN MIND**
> The product of multiplying a fraction by a fraction is always less than 1.

Examples

1. **Multiply $\frac{1}{2} \times \frac{3}{4}$.**

   A. $\frac{1}{4}$ B. $\frac{1}{2}$ C. $\frac{3}{8}$ D. $\frac{2}{3}$

   The correct answer is **C**. The correct solution is $\frac{3}{8}$ because $\frac{1}{2} \times \frac{3}{4} = \frac{3}{8}$.

2. **Multiply $\frac{2}{3} \times \frac{5}{6}$.**

   A. $\frac{1}{9}$ B. $\frac{5}{18}$ C. $\frac{5}{9}$ D. $\frac{7}{18}$

   The correct answer is **C**. The correct solution is $\frac{5}{9}$ because $\frac{2}{3} \times \frac{5}{6} = \frac{10}{18} = \frac{5}{9}$.

Multiply a Fraction by a Whole or Mixed Number

Multiplying a fraction by a whole or mixed number is similar to multiplying two fractions. When multiplying by a whole number, change the whole number to a fraction with a denominator of 1. Next, multiply the numerators together and the denominators together. Rewrite the final answer as a mixed number. For example: $\frac{9}{10} \times 3 = \frac{9}{10} \times \frac{3}{1} = \frac{27}{10} = 2\frac{7}{10}$.

When multiplying a fraction by a mixed number or multiplying two mixed numbers, the process is similar.

For example, multiply $\frac{10}{11} \times 3\frac{1}{2}$. Change the mixed number to an improper fraction, $\frac{10}{11} \times \frac{7}{2}$. Multiply the numerators together and multiply

> **KEEP IN MIND**
> Always change a mixed number to an improper fraction when multiplying by a mixed number.

the denominators together, $\frac{70}{22}$. Write the improper fraction as a mixed number, $3\frac{4}{22}$. Reduce if necessary, $3\frac{2}{11}$.

This process can also be used when multiplying a whole number by a mixed number or multiplying two mixed numbers.

Examples

1. **Multiply $4 \times \frac{5}{6}$.**

   A. $\frac{5}{24}$ B. $2\frac{3}{4}$ C. $3\frac{1}{3}$ D. $4\frac{5}{6}$

   The correct answer is **C**. The correct solution is $3\frac{1}{3}$ because $\frac{4}{1} \times \frac{5}{6} = \frac{20}{6} = 3\frac{2}{6} = 3\frac{1}{3}$.

2. **Multiply $1\frac{1}{2} \times 1\frac{1}{6}$.**

   A. $1\frac{1}{12}$ B. $1\frac{1}{4}$ C. $1\frac{3}{8}$ D. $1\frac{3}{4}$

   The correct answer is **D**. The correct solution is $1\frac{3}{4}$ because $\frac{3}{2} \times \frac{7}{6} = \frac{21}{12} = 1\frac{9}{12} = 1\frac{3}{4}$.

Dividing a Fraction by a Fraction

Some basic steps apply when dividing a fraction by a fraction. The information from the previous two sections is applicable to dividing fractions.

STEP BY STEP

Step 1. Leave the first fraction alone.

Step 2. Find the reciprocal of the second fraction.

Step 3. Multiply the first fraction by the reciprocal of the second fraction.

Step 4. Rewrite the fraction as a mixed number and reduce the fraction completely.

Divide, $\frac{3}{10} \div \frac{1}{2}$. Find the reciprocal of the second fraction, which is $\frac{2}{1}$.

Now, multiply the fractions, $\frac{3}{10} \times \frac{2}{1} = \frac{6}{10}$. Reduce $\frac{6}{10}$ to $\frac{3}{5}$.

Divide, $\frac{4}{5} \div \frac{3}{8}$. Find the reciprocal of the second fraction, which is $\frac{8}{3}$.

Now, multiply the fractions, $\frac{4}{5} \times \frac{8}{3} = \frac{32}{15}$. Rewrite the fraction as a mixed number, $\frac{32}{15} = 2\frac{2}{15}$.

Examples

1. **Divide $\frac{1}{2} \div \frac{5}{6}$.**

   A. $\frac{5}{12}$ B. $\frac{3}{5}$ C. $\frac{5}{6}$ D. $1\frac{2}{3}$

   The correct answer is **B**. The correct solution is $\frac{3}{5}$ because $\frac{1}{2} \times \frac{6}{5} = \frac{6}{10} = \frac{3}{5}$.

2. **Divide $\frac{2}{3} \div \frac{3}{5}$.**

   A. $\frac{2}{15}$ B. $\frac{2}{5}$ C. $1\frac{1}{15}$ D. $1\frac{1}{9}$

   The correct answer is **D**. The correct solution is $1\frac{1}{9}$ because $\frac{2}{3} \times \frac{5}{3} = \frac{10}{9} = 1\frac{1}{9}$.

Dividing a Fraction and a Whole or Mixed Number

Some basic steps apply when dividing a fraction by a whole number or a mixed number.

STEP BY STEP

Step 1. Write any whole number as a fraction with a denominator of 1. Write any mixed numbers as improper fractions.

Step 2. Leave the first fraction (improper fraction) alone.

Step 3. Find the reciprocal of the second fraction.

Step 4. Multiply the first fraction by the reciprocal of the second fraction.

Step 5. Rewrite the fraction as a mixed number and reduce the fraction completely.

Divide, $\frac{3}{10} \div 3$. Rewrite the expression as $\frac{3}{10} \div \frac{3}{1}$. Find the reciprocal of the second fraction, which is $\frac{1}{3}$. Multiply the fractions, $\frac{3}{10} \times \frac{1}{3} = \frac{3}{30} = \frac{1}{10}$. Reduce $\frac{3}{30}$ to $\frac{1}{10}$.

Divide, $2\frac{4}{5} \div 1\frac{3}{8}$. Rewrite the expression as $\frac{14}{5} \div \frac{11}{8}$. Find the reciprocal of the second fraction, which is $\frac{8}{11}$.

Multiply the fractions, $\frac{14}{5} \times \frac{8}{11} = \frac{112}{55} = 2\frac{2}{55}$. Reduce $\frac{112}{55}$ to $2\frac{2}{55}$.

Examples

1. **Divide $\frac{2}{3} \div 4$.**

   A. $\frac{1}{12}$ B. $\frac{1}{10}$ C. $\frac{1}{8}$ D. $\frac{1}{6}$

   The correct answer is **D**. The correct answer is $\frac{1}{6}$ because $\frac{2}{3} \times \frac{1}{4} = \frac{2}{12} = \frac{1}{6}$.

2. **Divide $1\frac{5}{12} \div 1\frac{1}{2}$.**

   A. $\frac{17}{18}$ B. $1\frac{5}{24}$ C. $1\frac{5}{6}$ D. $2\frac{1}{8}$

   The correct answer is **A**. The correct answer is $\frac{17}{18}$ because $\frac{17}{12} \div \frac{3}{2} = \frac{17}{12} \times \frac{2}{3} = \frac{34}{36} = \frac{17}{18}$.

Let's Review!

- The process to multiply fractions is to multiply the numerators together and multiply the denominators together. When there is a mixed number, change the mixed number to an improper fraction before multiplying.

- The process to divide fractions is to find the reciprocal of the second fraction and multiply the fractions. As with multiplying, change any mixed numbers to improper fractions before dividing.

RATIOS, PROPORTIONS, AND PERCENTAGES

This lesson reviews percentages and ratios and their application to real-world problems. It also examines proportions and rates of change.

Percentages

A **percent** or **percentage** represents a fraction of some quantity. It is an integer or decimal number followed by the symbol %. The word *percent* means "per hundred." For example, 50% means 50 per 100. This is equivalent to half, or 1 out of 2.

Converting between numbers and percents is easy. Given a number, multiply by 100 and add the % symbol to get the equivalent percent. For instance, 0.67 is equal to $0.67 \times 100 = 67\%$, meaning 67 out of 100. Given a percent, eliminate the % symbol and divide by 100. For instance, 23.5% is equal to $23.5 \div 100 = 0.235$.

Although percentages between 0% and 100% are the most obvious, a percent can be any real number, including a negative number. For example, $1.35 = 135\%$ and $-0.872 = -87.2\%$. An example is a gasoline tank that is one-quarter full: one-quarter is $\frac{1}{4}$ or 0.25, so the tank is 25% full. Another example is a medical diagnostic test that has a certain maximum normal result. If a patient's test exceeds that value, its representation can be a percent greater than 100%. For instance, a reading that is 1.22 times the maximum normal value is 122% of the maximum normal value. Likewise, when measuring increases in a company's profits as a percent from one year to the next, a negative percent can represent a decline. That is, if the company's profits fell by one-tenth, the change was −10%.

Example

If 15 out of every 250 contest entries are winners, what percentage of entries are winners?

A. 0.06%   B. 6%   C. 15%   D. 17%

The correct answer is **B**. First, convert the fraction $\frac{15}{250}$ to a decimal: 0.06. To get the percent, multiply by 100% (that is, multiply by 100 and add the % symbol). Of all entries, 6% are winners.

Ratios

A **ratio** expresses the relationship between two numbers and is expressed using a colon or fraction notation. For instance, if 135 runners finish a marathon but 22 drop out, the ratio of finishers to non-finishers is 135:22 or $\frac{135}{22}$. These expressions are equal.

> **BE CAREFUL!**
>
> Avoid confusing standard ratios with odds (such as "3:1 odds"). Both may use a colon, but their meanings differ. In general, a ratio is the same as a fraction containing the same numbers.

Ratios also follow the rules of fractions. Performing arithmetic operations on ratios follows the same procedures as on fractions. Ratios should also generally appear in lowest terms. Therefore, the constituent numbers in a ratio represent the relative quantities of each side, not absolute quantities. For example, because the ratio 1:2 is equal to 2:4, 5:10, and 600:1,200, ratios are insufficient to determine the absolute number of entities in a problem.

Example

If the ratio of women to men in a certain industry is 5:4, how many people are in that industry?

A. 9   B. 20   C. 900   D. Not enough information

The correct answer is **D**. The ratio 5:4 is the industry's relative number of women to men. But the industry could have 10 women and 8 men, 100 women and 80 men, or any other breakdown whose ratio is 5:4. Therefore, the question provides too little information to answer. Had it provided the total number of people in the industry, it would have been possible to determine how many women and how many men are in the industry.

> **KEY POINT**
> Mathematically, ratios act just like fractions. For example, the ratio 8:13 is mathematically the same as the fraction $\frac{8}{13}$.

Proportions

A **proportion** is an equation of two ratios. An illustrative case is two equivalent fractions:

$$\frac{21}{28} = \frac{3}{4}$$

This example of a proportion should be familiar: going left to right, it is the conversion of one fraction to an equivalent fraction in lowest terms by dividing the numerator and denominator by the same number (7, in this case).

Equating fractions in this way is correct, but it provides little information. Proportions are more informative when one of the numbers is unknown. Using a question mark (?) to represent an unknown number, setting up a proportion can aid in solving problems involving different scales. For instance, if the ratio of maple saplings to oak saplings in an acre of young forest is 7:5 and that acre contains 65 oaks, the number of maples in that acre can be determined using a proportion:

$$\frac{7}{5} = \frac{?}{65}$$

Note that to equate two ratios in this manner, the numerators must contain numbers that represent the same entity or type, and so must the denominators. In this example, the numerators represent maples and the denominators represent oaks.

$$\frac{7 \text{ maples}}{5 \text{ oaks}} = \frac{? \text{ maples}}{65 \text{ oaks}}$$

Recall from the properties of fractions that if you multiply the numerator and denominator by the same number, the result is an equivalent fraction. Therefore, to find the unknown in this proportion, first divide the denominator on the right by the denominator on the left. Then, multiply the quotient by the numerator on the left.

$$65 \div 5 = 13$$

$$\frac{7 \times 13}{5 \times 13} = \frac{?}{65}$$

The unknown (?) is $7 \times 13 = 91$. In the example, the acre of forest has 91 maple saplings.

> **DID YOU KNOW?**
>
> When taking the reciprocal of both sides of a proportion, the proportion still holds. When setting up a proportion, ensure that the numerators represent the same type and the denominators represent the same type.

Example

If a recipe calls for 3 parts flour to 2 parts sugar, how much sugar does a baker need if she uses 12 cups of flour?

   A. 2 cups   B. 3 cups   C. 6 cups   D. 8 cups

The correct answer is **D.** The baker needs 8 cups of sugar. First, note that "3 parts flour to 2 parts sugar" is the ratio 3:2. Set up the proportion using the given amount of flour (12 cups), putting the flour numbers in either the denominators or the numerators (either will yield the same answer):

$$\frac{3}{2} = \frac{12}{?}$$

Since $12 \div 3 = 4$, multiply 2×4 to get 8 cups of sugar.

Rates of Change

Numbers that describe current quantities can be informative, but how they change over time can provide even greater insight into a problem. The rate of change for some quantity is the ratio of the quantity's difference over a specific time period to the length of that period. For example, if an automobile increases its speed from 50 mph to 100 mph in 10 seconds, the rate of change of its speed (its acceleration) is

$$\frac{100\ \text{mph} - 50\ \text{mph}}{10\ \text{s}} = \frac{50\ \text{mph}}{10\ \text{s}} = 5\ \text{mph per second} = 5\ \text{mph/s}$$

The basic formula for the rate of change of some quantity is $\frac{x_f - x_i}{t_f - t_i}$.

where t_f is the "final" (or ending) time and t_i is the "initial" (or starting) time. Also, x_f is the (final) quantity at (final) time t_f, and x_i is the (initial) quantity at (initial) time t_i. In the example above, the final time is 10 seconds and the initial time is 0 seconds—hence the omission of the initial time from the calculation.

According to the rules of fractions, multiplying the numerator and denominator by the same number yields an equivalent fraction, so you can reverse the order of the terms in the formula:

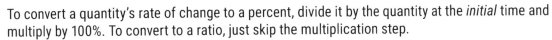

$$\frac{x_f - x_i}{t_f - t_i} = \frac{-1}{-1} \times \frac{x_f - x_i}{t_f - t_i} = \frac{x_i - x_f}{t_i - t_f}$$

The key to getting the correct rate of change is to ensure that the first number in the numerator and the first number in the denominator correspond to each other (that is, the quantity from the numerator corresponds to the time from the denominator). This must also be true for the second number.

TEST TIP

To convert a quantity's rate of change to a percent, divide it by the quantity at the *initial* time and multiply by 100%. To convert to a ratio, just skip the multiplication step.

Example

If the population of an endangered frog species fell from 2,250 individuals to 2,115 individuals in a year, what is that population's annual rate of increase?

A. −135%   B. −6%   C. 6%   D. 135%

The correct answer is **B**. The population's rate of increase was −6%. The solution in this case involves two steps. First, calculate the population's annual rate of change using the formula. It will yield the change in the number of individuals.

$$\frac{2,115 - 2,250}{1 \text{ year} - 0 \text{ year}} = -135 \text{ per year}$$

Second, divide the result by the initial population. Finally, convert to a percent.

$$\frac{-135 \text{ per year}}{2,250} = -0.06 \text{ per year}$$

$$(-0.06 \text{ per year}) \times 100\% = -6\% \text{ per year}$$

Since the question asks for the *annual* rate of increase, the "per year" can be dropped. Also, note that the answer must be negative to represent the decreasing population.

Let's Review!

- A percent—meaning "per hundred"—represents a relative quantity as a fraction or decimal. It is the absolute number multiplied by 100 and followed by the % symbol.
- A ratio is a relationship between two numbers expressed using fraction or colon notation (for example, $\frac{3}{2}$ or 3:2). Ratios behave mathematically just like fractions.
- An equation of two ratios is called a proportion. Proportions are used to solve problems involving scale.
- Rates of change are the speeds at which quantities increase or decrease. The formula $\frac{x_f - x_i}{t_f - t_i}$ provides the rate of change of quantity x over the period between some initial (i) time and final (f) time.

INTERPRETING CATEGORICAL AND QUANTITATIVE DATA

This lesson discusses how to represent and interpret data for a dot plot, a histogram, and a box plot. It compares multiple sets of data by using the measures of center and spread and examines the impact of outliers.

Representing Data on a Number Line

There are two types of data: quantitative and categorical. Quantitative variables are numerical, such as number of people in a household, bank account balance, and number of cars sold. Categorical variables are not numerical, and there is no inherent way to order them. Example are classes in college, types of pets, and party affiliations. The information for these data sets can be arranged on a number line using dot plots, histograms, and box plots.

A dot plot is a display of data using dots. The dots represent the number of times an item appears. Below is a sample of a dot plot.

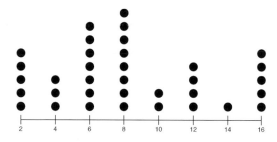

The mean and median can be determined by looking at a dot plot. The mean is the sum of all items divided by the number of dots. The median is the middle dot or the average of the middle two dots.

A histogram is a graphical display that has bars of various heights. It is similar to a bar chart, but the numbers are grouped into ranges. The bins, or ranges of values, of a histogram have equal lengths, such as 10 or 50 units. Continuous data such as weight, height, and amount of time are examples of data shown in a histogram. In the histogram to the right, the bin length is 8 units.

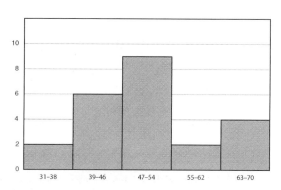

It is not possible to calculate the mean and median by looking at a histogram because there is a bin size rather than a single value on the horizontal axis. Histograms are beneficial when working with a large set of data.

A box plot (or box-and-whisker plot) is a graphical display of the minimum, first quartile, median, third quartile, and maximum of a set of data.

BE CAREFUL!

Make sure to carefully interpret the data for any graphical display.

Recall the minimum is the smallest value and the maximum is the largest value in a set of data. The median is the middle number when the data set is written in order. The first quartile is the middle number between the minimum and the median. The third quartile is the middle number between the median and the maximum.

In the data display below, the minimum is 45, the first quartile is 50, the median is 57, the third quartile is 63, and the maximum is 75. With most box-and-whisker plots, the data is not symmetrical.

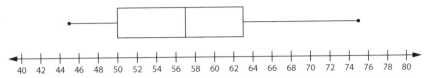

Example

The histogram below shows a basketball team's winning margin during the season. Which statement is true for the histogram?

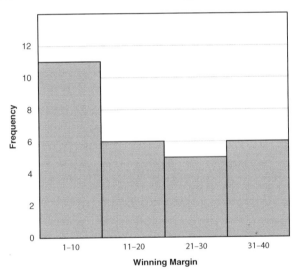

A. The team played a total of 30 games.

B. The frequency for 20–30 points is the same as for 30–40 points.

C. The sum of the frequency for the last two bins is the same as the first bin.

D. The frequency for 0–10 is twice the frequency for any other winning margin.

The correct answer is **C**. The correct solution is the sum of the frequency for the last two bins is the same as the first bin. The frequency of the first bin is 11, the frequency of the third bin is 5, and the frequency of the fourth bin is 6. The sum of the frequency of the last two bins is the same as the first bin.

Comparing Center and Spread of Multiple Data Sets

The measures of center are the mean (average) and median (middle number when written in order). These values describe the expected value of a data set. Very large or very small numbers affect the mean, but they do not affect the median.

The measures of spread are standard deviation (how far the numbers of a data set are from the mean) and interquartile range (the difference between the third and first quartile values).

To find the standard deviation:

- Find the mean.
- Find the difference between the mean and each member of the date set and square that result.
- Find the mean of the squared differences from the previous step.
- Apply the square root.

The larger the value for the standard deviation, the greater the spread of values from the mean. The larger the value for the interquartile range, the greater the spread of the middle 50% of values from the median.

Symmetric data has values that are close together, and the mean, median, and mode occur near the same value. The mean and standard deviation are used to explain multiple data sets and are evident in dot plots.

For example, consider this data set.

10, 10, 11, 11, 11, 12, 12, 12, 12, 12, 13, 13, 13, 14, 14

The mean is found by finding the sum of the numbers in the data set and dividing it by the number of items in the set, as follows:

$10 + 10 + 11 + 11 + 11 + 12 + 12 + 12 + 12 + 12 + 13 + 13 + 13 + 14 + 14 = 180 \div 15 = 12.$

The standard deviation calculation is shown in the table below.

Data	Data − Mean	(Data − Mean)^2
10	−2	4
10	−2	4
11	−1	1
11	−1	1
11	−1	1
12	0	0
12	0	0
12	0	0

Data	Data − Mean	(Data − Mean)^2
12	0	0
12	0	0
13	1	1
13	1	1
13	1	1
14	2	4
14	2	4

The sum of the last column is 22. The standard deviation is $\sqrt{\frac{22}{15}} \approx 1.211$.

Next, consider this data set.

8, 8, 9, 10, 11, 12, 12, 12, 12, 12, 13, 14, 15, 16, 16

The mean is $8 + 8 + 9 + 10 + 11 + 12 + 12 + 12 + 12 + 12 + 13 + 14 + 15 + 16 + 16 = 180 \div 15 = 12$.

The standard deviation calculation is shown in the table below.

Data	Data − Mean	(Data − Mean)^2
8	−4	16
8	−4	16
9	−3	9
10	−2	4
11	−1	1
12	0	0
12	0	0
12	0	0

Data	Data − Mean	(Data − Mean)^2
12	0	0
12	0	0
13	1	1
14	2	4
15	3	9
16	4	16
16	4	16

The sum of the last column is 92. The standard deviation is $\sqrt{\frac{92}{15}} \approx 2.476$.

Therefore, the second set of data has values that are farther from the mean than the first data set.

When data is skewed, a group of its values are close and the remaining values are evenly spread. The median and interquartile range are used to explain multiple data sets and are evident in dot plots and box plots.

KEEP IN MIND

Compare the same measure of center or variation to draw accurate conclusions when comparing data sets.

The data set 10, 10, 11, 11, 11, 11, 11, 11, 12, 12, 12, 13, 13, 14, 15 has a median of 11 and an interquartile range of 2. The data set 10, 11, 12, 12, 13, 13, 14, 14, 14, 14, 14, 14, 14, 15, 15 has a median of 14 and an interquartile range of 2. The median is greater in the second data set, but the spread of data is the same for both sets of data.

Example

The box plots below show the heights of students in inches for two classes. Choose the statement that is true for the median and the interquartile range.

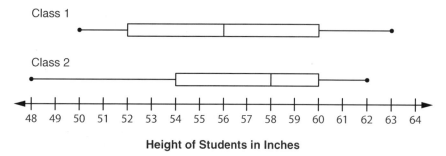

Height of Students in Inches

A. The median and interquartile range are greater for class 1.

B. The median and interquartile range are greater for class 2.

C. The median is greater for class 1, and the interquartile range is greater for class 2.

D. The median is greater for class 2, and the interquartile range is greater for class 1.

The correct answer is **D**. The correct solution is the median is greater for class 2, and the interquartile range is greater for class 1. The median is 58 inches for class 2 and 56 inches for class 1. The interquartile range is 8 inches for class 1 and 6 inches for class 2.

Determining the Effect of Extreme Data Points

An outlier is a value that is much smaller or much larger than rest of the values in a data set. This value has an impact on the mean and standard deviation values and occasionally has an impact on the median and interquartile range values.

The data set of 10, 10, 11, 11, 11, 12, 12, 12, 12, 12, 13, 13, 13, 14, 14 has a mean of 12 and a standard deviation of 1.211. If an outlier of 50 is added, the data set has a mean of has a mean of 14.38 and a standard deviation of 9.273. The outlier has

BE CAREFUL!

There may be a high outlier and a low outlier that may not have an impact on data.

increased the mean by more than 2, and the spread of the data has increased significantly.

The data set 10, 10, 11, 11, 11, 11, 11, 11, 12, 12, 12, 13, 13, 14, 15 has a median of 11 and an interquartile range of 2. If an outlier of 50 is added, the median slightly increases to 11.5 and the interquartile range remains 2.

Example

A little league basketball team scores 35, 38, 40, 36, 41, 42, 39, 35, 29, 32, 37, 33 in its first 12 games. In its next game, the team scores 12 points. Which statement describes the mean and standard deviation?

    A. The mean increases, and the standard deviation increases.

    B. The mean decreases, and the standard deviation increases.

    C. The mean increases, and the standard deviation decreases.

    D. The mean decreases, and the standard deviation decreases.

The correct answer is **B**. The correct solution is the mean decreases, and the standard deviation increases. The outlier value is lower than all other values, which results in a decrease for the mean. The standard deviation increases because the outlier of 12 is a value far away from the mean.

Let's Review!

- Dot plots, histograms, and box plots summarize and represent data on a number line.
- The mean and standard deviation are used to compare symmetric data sets.
- The median and interquartile range are used to compare skewed data sets.
- Outliers can impact measures of center and spread, particularly mean and standard deviation.

CHAPTER 1 NUMBERS AND BASIC OPERATIONS PRACTICE QUIZ 1

1. Which number is less than all the others?

   A. −223   C. 0

   B. −18   D. 223

2. What is 604 − 561?

   A. 34   C. 53

   B. 43   D. 143

3. Evaluate the expression (−224) ÷ 14.

   A. −210   C. 16

   B. −16   D. 210

4. Evaluate the expression −3 × 5.

   A. −15   C. 2

   B. −2   D. 15

5. Change $\frac{5}{11}$ to a decimal. Simplify completely.

   A. $0.\overline{4}$ C. $0.\overline{5}$

   B. $0.\overline{45}$ D. $0.\overline{54}$

6. Which decimal is the least?

   A. 5.2304   C. 5.2403

   B. 5.3204   D. 5.3024

7. The data below show the number of cars that drove through an intersection on a Saturday.

   1, 48, 60, 43, 41, 70, 75, 80, 101, 90, 121, 114, 99, 153, 205, 175, 222, 96, 201, 158, 141, 117, 74, 29

Select a histogram for the data.

A.

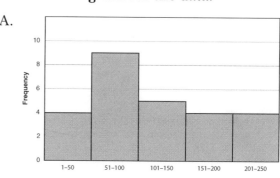

B.

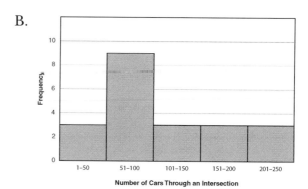

C.

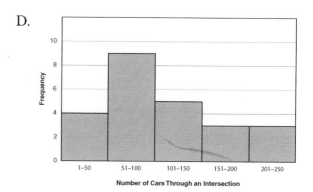

D.

8. Find the median from the dot plot.

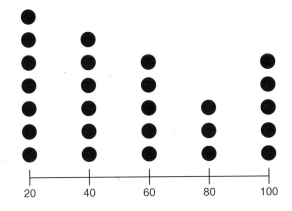

A. 40

B. 50

C. 60

D. 70

9. Multiply $5\frac{1}{2} \times \frac{7}{8}$.

A. $4\frac{3}{10}$

B. $4\frac{13}{16}$

C. $5\frac{7}{16}$

D. $5\frac{7}{10}$

10. Divide $\frac{5}{7} \div \frac{4}{7}$.

A. $\frac{1}{7}$

B. $\frac{4}{5}$

C. $1\frac{1}{4}$

D. $7\frac{4}{5}$

11. If a recipe calls for 3 parts flour to 2 parts sugar, how much sugar does a baker need if she uses 12 cups of flour?

A. 2 cups

B. 3 cups

C. 6 cups

D. 8 cups

12. What is the product of 3:2 and 5:6?

A. 4:5

B. 1:1

C. 5:4

D. 9:5

CHAPTER 1 NUMBERS AND BASIC OPERATIONS PRACTICE QUIZ 1 – ANSWER KEY

1. A. The correct solution is −223. A negative number is always less than a positive number. Also, a negative number is less than another negative number if it is farther left on the number line: here, −223 < −18. **See Lesson: Basic Addition and Subtraction.**

2. B. The correct solution is 43. Use the subtraction algorithm, which will require borrowing once. **See Lesson: Basic Addition and Subtraction.**

3. B. When dividing signed numbers, remember that if the dividend and divisor have different signs, the quotient is negative. Other than the sign, the process is the same as dividing whole numbers. Use the division algorithm to divide 224 by 14. **See Lesson: Basic Multiplication and Division.**

4. A. When multiplying signed numbers, remember that the product of a negative and a positive is negative. Other than the sign, the process is the same as multiplying whole numbers. **See Lesson: Basic Multiplication and Division.**

5. B. The correct answer is $0.\overline{45}$ because $\frac{5}{11} = 5.00 \div 11 = 0.\overline{45}$. **See Lesson: Decimals and Fractions.**

6. A. The correct solution is 5.2304 because 5.2304 contains the smallest value in the tenths and the hundredths places. **See Lesson: Decimals and Fractions.**

7. B. The correct solution is B. Each bin contains 50 cars, and the frequencies are 4, 9, 5, 3, and 3. **See Lesson: Interpreting Categorical and Quantitative Data.**

8. B. The correct solution is 50. The middle two values are 40 and 60, and the average of these values is 50. **See Lesson: Interpreting Categorical and Quantitative Data.**

9. B. The correct solution is $4\frac{13}{16}$ because $\frac{11}{2} \times \frac{7}{8} = \frac{77}{16} = 4\frac{13}{16}$. **See Lesson: Multiplication and Division of Fractions.**

10. C. The correct solution is $1\frac{1}{4}$ because $\frac{5}{7} \times \frac{7}{4} = \frac{35}{28} = 1\frac{7}{28} = 1\frac{1}{4}$. **See Lesson: Multiplication and Division of Fractions.**

11. D. The baker needs 8 cups of sugar. First, note that "3 parts flour to 2 parts sugar" is the ratio 3:2. Set up the proportion using the given amount of flour (12 cups), putting the flour numbers in either the denominators or the numerators (either will yield the same answer): $\frac{3}{2} = \frac{12}{?}$ Since 12 ÷ 3 = 4, multiply 2 × 4 to get 8 cups of sugar. **See Lesson: Ratios, Proportions, and Percentages.**

12. C. The correct answer is C. Ratios act just like fractions, so this product is the product of $\frac{3}{2}$ and $\frac{5}{6}$, or $\frac{15}{12} = \frac{5}{4}$. **See Lesson: Ratios, Proportions, and Percentages.**

CHAPTER 1 NUMBERS AND BASIC OPERATIONS PRACTICE QUIZ 2

1. A biologist has captured only two kinds of snakes, ringnecks and garters. If she has 6 ringneck snakes and 13 snakes total, how many garter snakes does she have?

   A. 6

   B. 7

   C. 13

   D. 19

2. Place the following numbers in order from greatest to least: 5, −12, 0.

   A. 0, 5, −12

   B. −12, 5, 0

   C. 5, 0, −12

   D. −12, 0, 5

3. What is $96 \div 12$?

   A. 8

   B. 84

   C. 960

   D. 1,152

4. Given an expression with no parentheses, which should be evaluated first?

   A. Division

   B. Addition

   C. Subtraction

   D. Any of the above

5. Which fraction is the least?

   A. $\frac{1}{4}$

   B. $\frac{1}{2}$

   C. $\frac{5}{16}$

   D. $\frac{3}{8}$

6. Change $7\frac{13}{20}$ to a decimal. Simplify completely.

   A. 7.55

   B. 7.6

   C. 7.65

   D. 7.7

7. A basketball player scores 18, 17, 20, 23, 15, 24, 22, 28, 5. What is the effect of removing the outlier on the mean and standard deviation?

   A. The mean and the standard deviation increase.

   B. The mean and the standard deviation decrease.

   C. The standard deviation increases, but the mean decreases.

   D. The standard deviation decreases, but the mean increases.

8. The data below shows the number of minutes available to eat breakfast for a group of employees.

   10, 20, 40, 30, 50, 60, 50, 40, 30, 20, 40, 30, 10, 20, 30, 50, 40, 10, 10, 20, 30, 40, 20, 50, 40, 30

   Select a dot plot for the data.

A.   **Minutes to Eat Breakfast**

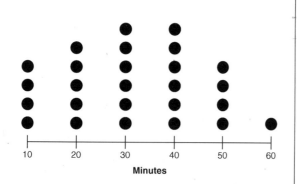

C.   **Minutes to Eat Breakfast**

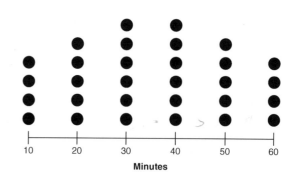

B.   **Minutes to Eat Breakfast**

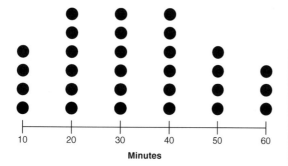

D.   **Minutes to Eat Breakfast**

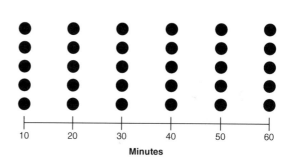

9. Multiply $\frac{3}{16} \times \frac{4}{7}$.

    A. $\frac{3}{28}$ C. $\frac{1}{6}$

    B. $\frac{1}{9}$ D. $\frac{7}{9}$

10. Multiply $3\frac{1}{5} \times \frac{5}{8}$.

    A. 1   C. 3

    B. 2   D. 4

11. If 15 out of every 250 contest entries are winners, what percentage of entries are winners?

    A. 0.06%   C. 15%

    B. 6%   D. 17%

12. Which percent is closest to the ratio 7:3?

    A. 23%   C. 73%

    B. 43%   D. 233%

CHAPTER 1 NUMBERS AND BASIC OPERATIONS PRACTICE QUIZ 2 – ANSWER KEY

1. B. The correct solution is 7. Since the biologist only has ringnecks and garters, any snake in her possession is a garter if it is not a ringneck. Because she has 13 snakes but 6 ringneck snakes, the number of garter snakes is the difference: 13 – 6 = 7. **See Lesson: Basic Addition and Subtraction.**

2. C. The correct solution is 5, 0, –12. Use the number line to order the numbers. Note that the question says *from greatest to least.* **See Lesson: Basic Addition and Subtraction.**

3. A. Use the division algorithm. Knowing the multiplication table well helps you recognize these numbers. **See Lesson: Basic Multiplication and Division.**

4. A. The order of operations (recall the mnemonic PEMDAS) requires multiplication and division before addition and subtraction. **See Lesson: Basic Multiplication and Division.**

5. A. The correct solution is $\frac{1}{4}$ because $\frac{1}{4}$ has the smallest numerator when comparing to the other fractions with the same denominator. The fractions with a common denominator of 16 are $\frac{1}{4} = \frac{4}{16}, \frac{1}{2} = \frac{8}{16}, \frac{5}{16} = \frac{5}{16}, \frac{3}{8} = \frac{6}{16}$. **See Lesson: Decimals and Fractions.**

6. C. The correct answer is 7.65 because $\frac{13}{20} = 13.00 \div 20 = 0.65$. **See Lesson: Decimals and Fractions.**

7. D. The correct solution is the standard deviation decreases, but the mean increases. The standard deviation from 6.226 and 3.951 when the low outlier is removed. The mean increases from 19.11 to 20.88 because the outlier, 5, is the lowest value. **See Lesson: Interpreting Categorical and Quantitative Data.**

8. A. The correct solution is A. There are 4 employees who have 10 minutes and 50 minutes, 5 employees who have 20 minutes, 6 employees who have 30 minutes and 40 minutes, and 1 employee who has 60 minutes. **See Lesson: Interpreting Categorical and Quantitative Data.**

9. A. The correct solution is $\frac{3}{28}$ because $\frac{3}{16} \times \frac{4}{7} = \frac{12}{112} = \frac{3}{28}$. **See Lesson: Multiplication and Division of Fractions.**

10. B. The correct solution is 2 because $\frac{16}{5} \times \frac{5}{8} = \frac{80}{40} = 2$. **See Lesson: Multiplication and Division of Fractions.**

11. B. First, convert the fraction $\frac{15}{250}$ to a decimal: 0.06. To get the percent, multiply by 100% (that is, multiply by 100 and add the % symbol). Of all entries, 6% are winners. **See Lesson: Ratios, Proportions, and Percentages.**

12. D. To convert a ratio to a percent, divide the numbers in the ratio (noting that its equivalent fraction is $\frac{7}{3}$) to get approximately 2.33. Then, multiply by 100%. **See Lesson: Ratios, Proportions, and Percentages.**

CHAPTER 2 ALGEBRA

EQUATIONS WITH ONE VARIABLE

This lesson introduces how to solve linear equations and linear inequalities.

One-Step Linear Equations

A **linear equation** is an equation where two expressions are set equal to each other. The equation is in the form $ax + b = c$, where a is a non-zero constant and b and c are constants. The exponent on a linear equation is always 1, and there is no more than one solution to a linear equation.

There are four properties to help solve a linear equation.

Property	Definition	Example with Numbers	Example with Variables
Addition Property of Equality	Add the same number to both sides of the equation.	$x-3 = 9$ $x-3 + 3 = 9 + 3$ $x = 12$	$x-a = b$ $x-a + a = b + a$ $x = a + b$
Subtraction Property of Equality	Subtract the same number from both sides of the equation.	$x + 3 = 9$ $x + 3-3 = 9-3$ $x = 6$	$x + a = b$ $x + a-a = b-a$ $x = b-a$
Multiplication Property of Equality	Multiply both sides of the equation by the same number.	$\frac{x}{3} = 9$ $\frac{x}{3} \times 3 = 9 \times 3$ $x = 27$	$\frac{x}{a} = b$ $\frac{x}{a} \times a = b \times a$ $x = ab$
Division Property of Equality	Divide both sides of the equation by the same number.	$3x = 9$ $\frac{3x}{3} = \frac{9}{3}$ $x = 3$	$ax = b$ $\frac{ax}{a} = \frac{b}{a}$ $x = \frac{b}{a}$

Example

Solve the equation for the unknown, $\frac{w}{2} = -6$.

A. −12   B. −8   C. −4   D. −3

The correct answer is **A**. The correct solution is −12 because both sides of the equation are multiplied by 2.

Two-Step Linear Equations

A two-step linear equation is in the form $ax + b = c$, where a is a non-zero constant and b and c are constants. There are two basic steps in solving this equation.

> **STEP BY STEP**
>
> **Step 1.** Use addition and subtraction properties of an equation to move the variable to one side of the equation and all number terms to the other side of the equation.
>
> **Step 2.** Use multiplication and division properties of an equation to remove the value in front of the variable.

Examples

1. **Solve the equation for the unknown, $\frac{x}{-2} - 3 = 5$.**

    A. −16   B. −8   C. 8   D. 16

    The correct answer is **A**. The correct solution is −16.

$\frac{x}{-2} = 8$	Add 3 to both sides of the equation.
$x = -16$	Multiply both sides of the equation by −2.

2. **Solve the equation for the unknown, $4x + 3 = 8$.**

    A. −2   B. $-\frac{5}{4}$ C. $\frac{5}{4}$ D. 2

    The correct answer is **C**. The correct solution is $\frac{5}{4}$.

$4x = 5$	Subtract 3 from both sides of the equation.
$x = \frac{5}{4}$	Divide both sides of the equation by 4.

3. **Solve the equation for the unknown w, $P = 2l + 2w$.**

    A. $2P{-}2l = w$ B. $\frac{P{-}2l}{2} = w$ C. $2P + 2l = w$ D. $\frac{P + 2l}{2} = w$

    The correct answer is **B**. The correct solution is $\frac{P{-}2l}{2} = w$.

$P{-}2l = 2w$	Subtract 2l from both sides of the equation.
$\frac{P{-}2l}{2} = w$	Divide both sides of the equation by 2.

Multi-Step Linear Equations

In these basic examples of linear equations, the solution may be evident, but these properties demonstrate how to use an opposite operation to solve for a variable. Using these properties, there are three steps in solving a complex linear equation.

> **STEP BY STEP**
>
> **Step 1.** Simplify each side of the equation. This includes removing parentheses, removing fractions, and adding like terms.
>
> **Step 2.** Use addition and subtraction properties of an equation to move the variable to one side of the equation and all number terms to the other side of the equation.
>
> **Step 3.** Use multiplication and division properties of an equation to remove the value in front of the variable.

In Step 2, all of the variables may be placed on the left side or the right side of the equation. The examples in this lesson will place all of the variables on the left side of the equation.

When solving for a variable, apply the same steps as above. In this case, the equation is not being solved for a value, but for a specific variable.

Examples

1. **Solve the equation for the unknown, $2(4x + 1)-5 = 3-(4x - 3)$.**

    A. $\frac{1}{4}$ B. $\frac{3}{4}$ C. $\frac{4}{3}$ D. 4

    The correct answer is **B**. The correct solution is $\frac{3}{4}$.

$8x + 2-5 = 3-4x + 3$	Apply the distributive property.
$8x-3 = -4x + 6$	Combine like terms on both sides of the equation.
$12x-3 = 6$	Add $4x$ to both sides of the equation.
$12x = 9$	Add 3 to both sides of the equation.
$x = \frac{3}{4}$	Divide both sides of the equation by 12.

2. **Solve the equation for the unknown, $\frac{2}{3}x + 2 = -\frac{1}{2}x + 2(x + 1)$.**

    A. 0 B. 1 C. 2 D. 3

    The correct answer is **A**. The correct solution is 0.

$\frac{2}{3}x + 2 = -\frac{1}{2}x + 2x + 2$	Apply the distributive property.
$4x + 12 = -3x + 12x + 12$	Multiply all terms by the least common denominator of 6 to eliminate the fractions.
$4x + 12 = 9x + 12$	Combine like terms on the right side of the equation.
$-5x = 12$	Subtract $9x$ from both sides of the equation.
$-5x = 0$	Subtract 12 from both sides of the equation.
$x = 0$	Divide both sides of the equation by -5.

3. **Solve the equation for the unknown for x, $y-y_1 = m(x-x_1)$.**

    A. $y-y_1 + mx_1$ B. $my - my_1 + mx_1$ C. $\frac{y-y_1 + x_1}{m}$ D. $\frac{y-y_1 + mx_1}{m}$

    The correct answer is **D**. The correct solution is $\frac{y-y_1 + mx_1}{m}$.

$y-y_1 = mx-mx_1$	Apply the distributive property.
$y-y_1 + mx_1 = mx$	Add mx_1 to both sides of the equation.
$\frac{y-y_1 + mx_1}{m} = x$	Divide both sides of the equation by m.

Solving Linear Inequalities

A **linear inequality** is similar to a linear equation, but it contains an inequality sign ($<, >, \leq, \geq$). Many of the steps for solving linear inequalities are the same as for solving linear equations.

The major difference is that the solution is an infinite number of values. There are four properties to help solve a linear inequality.

Property	Definition	Example
Addition Property of Inequality	Add the same number to both sides of the inequality.	$x-3 < 9$ $x-3+3 < 9+3$ $x < 12$
Subtraction Property of Inequality	Subtract the same number from both sides of the inequality.	$x+3 > 9$ $x+3-3 > 9-3$ $x > 6$
Multiplication Property of Inequality (when multiplying by a positive number)	Multiply both sides of the inequality by the same number.	$\frac{x}{3} \geq 9$ $\frac{x}{3} \times 3 \geq 9 \times 3$ $x \geq 27$
Division Property of Inequality (when multiplying by a positive number)	Divide both sides of the inequality by the same number.	$3x \leq 9$ $\frac{3x}{3} \leq \frac{9}{3}$ $x \leq 3$
Multiplication Property of Inequality (when multiplying by a negative number)	Multiply both sides of the inequality by the same number.	$\frac{x}{-3} \geq 9$ $\frac{x}{-3} \times -3 \geq 9 \times -3$ $x \leq -27$
Division Property of Inequality (when multiplying by a negative number)	Divide both sides of the inequality by the same number.	$-3x \leq 9$ $\frac{-3x}{-3} \leq \frac{9}{-3}$ $x \geq -3$

Multiplying or dividing both sides of the inequality by a negative number reverses the sign of the inequality.

In these basic examples, the solution may be evident, but these properties demonstrate how to use an opposite operation to solve for a variable. Using these properties, there are three steps in solving a complex linear inequality.

STEP BY STEP

Step 1. Simplify each side of the inequality. This includes removing parentheses, removing fractions, and adding like terms.

Step 2. Use addition and subtraction properties of an inequality to move the variable to one side of the equation and all number terms to the other side of the equation.

Step 3. Use multiplication and division properties of an inequality to remove the value in front of the variable. Reverse the inequality sign if multiplying or dividing by a negative number.

In Step 2, all of the variables may be placed on the left side or the right side of the inequality. The examples in this lesson will place all of the variables on the left side of the inequality.

Examples

1. **Solve the inequality for the unknown, $3(2 + x) < 2(3x-1)$.**

    A. $x < -\frac{8}{3}$ 　　　　 B. $x > -\frac{8}{3}$ 　　　　 C. $x < \frac{8}{3}$ 　　　　 D. $x > \frac{8}{3}$

    The correct answer is **D**. The correct solution is $x > \frac{8}{3}$.

$6 + 3x < 6x-2$	Apply the distributive property.
$6-3x < -2$	Subtract $6x$ from both sides of the inequality.
$-3x < -8$	Subtract 6 from both sides of the inequality.
$x > \frac{8}{3}$	Divide both sides of the inequality by 2.

2. **Solve the inequality for the unknown, $\frac{1}{2}(2x-3) \geq \frac{1}{4}(2x + 1)-2$.**

    A. $x > -7$ 　　　　 B. $x > -3$ 　　　　 C. $x \geq -\frac{3}{2}$ 　　　　 D. $x \geq -\frac{1}{2}$

    The correct answer is **D**. The correct solution is $x \geq -\frac{1}{2}$.

$2(2x-3) \geq 2x + 1-8$	Multiply all terms by the least common denominator of 4 to eliminate the fractions.
$4x-6 \geq 2x + 1-8$	Apply the distributive property.
$4x-6 \geq 2x-7$	Combine like terms on the right side of the inequality.
$2x-6 \geq -7$	Subtract $2x$ from both sides of the inequality.
$2x \geq -1$	Add 6 to both sides of the inequality.
$x \geq -\frac{1}{2}$	Divide both sides of the inequality by 3.

Let's Review!

-   A linear equation is an equation with one solution. Using opposite operations solves a linear equation.
-   The process to solve a linear equation or inequality is to eliminate fractions and parentheses and combine like terms on the same side of the sign. Then, solve the equation or inequality by using inverse operations.

EQUATIONS WITH TWO VARIABLES

This lesson discusses solving a system of linear equations by substitution, elimination, and graphing, as well as solving a simple system of a linear and a quadratic equation.

Solving a System of Equations by Substitution

A **system of linear equations** is a set of two or more linear equations in the same variables. A solution to the system is an ordered pair that is a solution in all the equations in the system. The ordered pair (1, -2) is a solution for the system of equations $\begin{matrix} 2x + y = 0 \\ -x + 2y = -5 \end{matrix}$ because $\begin{matrix} 2(1) + (-2) = 0 \\ -1 + 2(-2) = -5 \end{matrix}$ makes both equations true.

One way to solve a system of linear equations is by substitution.

> **STEP BY STEP**
>
> **Step 1.** Solve one equation for one of the variables.
>
> **Step 2.** Substitute the expression from Step 1 into the other equation and solve for the other variable.
>
> **Step 3.** Substitute the value from Step 2 into one of the original equations and solve.

All systems of equations can be solved by substitution for any one of the four variables in the problem. The most efficient way of solving is locating the $1x$ or $1y$ in the equations because this eliminates the possibility of having fractions in the equations.

Examples

1. **Solve the system of equations,** $\begin{matrix} x = y + 6 \\ 4x + 5y = 60 \end{matrix}$.

    A. (10, 12)   B. (6, 12)   C. (6, 4)   D. (10, 4)

    The correct answer is **D.** The correct solution is (10, 4).

    The first equation is already solved for x.

$4(y + 6) + 5y = 60$	Substitute $y + 6$ in for x in the first equation.
$4y + 24 + 5y = 60$	Apply the distributive property.
$9y + 24 = 60$	Combine like terms on the left side of the equation.
$9y = 36$	Subtract 24 from both sides of the equation.
$y = 4$	Divide both sides of the equation by 9.
$x = 4 + 6$	Substitute 4 in the first equation for y.
$x = 10$	Simplify using order of operations

2. **Solve the system of equations,** $\begin{array}{l} 3x + 2y = 41 \\ -4x + y = -18 \end{array}$.

   A. (5, 13)   B. (6, 6)   C. (7, 10)   D. (10, 7)

The correct answer is **C**. The correct solution is (7, 10).

$y = 4x{-}18$	Solve the second equation for y by adding $4x$ to both sides of the equation.
$3x + 2(4x{-}18) = 41$	Substitute $4x{-}18$ in for y in the first equation.
$3x + 8x{-}36 = 41$	Apply the distributive property.
$11x{-}36 = 41$	Combine like terms on the left side of the equation.
$11x = 77$	Add 36 to both sides of the equation.
$x = 7$	Divide both sides of the equation by 11.
$-4(7) + y = -18$	Substitute 7 in the second equation for x.
$-28 + y = -18$	Simplify using order of operations.
$y = 10$	Add 28 to both sides of the equation.

Solving a System of Equations by Elimination

Another way to solve a system of linear equations is by elimination.

STEP BY STEP

Step 1. Multiply, if necessary, one or both equations by a constant so at least one pair of like terms has opposite coefficients.

Step 2. Add the equations to eliminate one of the variables.

Step 3. Solve the resulting equation.

Step 4. Substitute the value from Step 3 into one of the original equations and solve for the other variable.

All system of equations can be solved by the elimination method for any one of the four variables in the problem. One way of solving is locating the variables with opposite coefficients and adding the equations. Another approach is multiplying one equation to obtain opposite coefficients for the variables.

Examples

1. **Solve the system of equations,** $\begin{array}{l} 3x + 5y = 28 \\ -4x-5y = -34 \end{array}$.

   A. $(12, 6)$ B. $(6, 12)$ C. $(6, 2)$ D. $(2, 6)$

   The correct answer is **C**. The correct solution is $(6, 2)$.

$-x = -6$	Add the equations.
$x = 6$	Divide both sides of the equation by -1.
$3(6) + 5y = 28$	Substitute 6 in the first equation for x.
$18 + 5y = 28$	Simplify using order of operations.
$5y = 10$	Subtract 18 from both sides of the equation.
$y = 2$	Divide both sides of the equation by 5.

2. **Solve the system of equations,** $\begin{array}{l} -5x + 5y = 0 \\ 2x-3y = -3 \end{array}$.

   A. $(2, 2)$ B. $(3, 3)$ C. $(6, 6)$ D. $(9, 9)$

   The correct answer is **B**. The correct solution is $(3, 3)$.

$-10x + 10y = 0$	Multiply all terms in the first equation by 2.
$10x-15y = -15$	Multiply all terms in the second equation by 5.
$-5y = -15$	Add the equations.
$y = 3$	Divide both sides of the equation by -5.
$2x-3(3) = -3$	Substitute 3 in the second equation for y.
$2x-9 = -3$	Simplify using order of operations.
$2x = 6$	Add 9 to both sides of the equation.
$x = 3$	Divide both sides of the equation by 2.

Solving a System of Equations by Graphing

Graphing is a third method of a solving system of equations. The point of intersection is the solution for the graph. This method is a great way to visualize each graph on a coordinate plane.

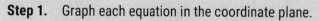

STEP BY STEP

Step 1. Graph each equation in the coordinate plane.

Step 2. Estimate the point of intersection.

Step 3. Check the point by substituting for x and y in each equation of the original system.

The best approach to graphing is to obtain each line in slope-intercept form. Then, graph the y-intercept and use the slope to find additional points on the line.

Example

Solve the system of equations by graphing, $\begin{matrix} y = 3x-2 \\ y = x-4 \end{matrix}$.

A.

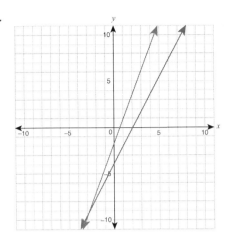

C.

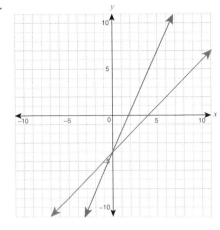

B.

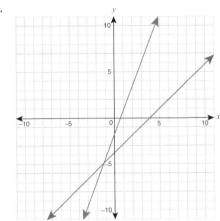

D.

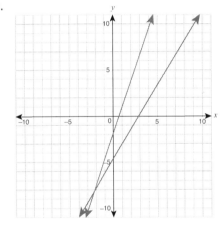

The correct answer is **B.** The correct graph has the two lines intersect at (-1, -5).

Solving a System of a Linear Equation and an Equation of a Circle

There are many other types of systems of equations. One example is the equation of a line $y = mx$ and the equation of a circle $x^2 + y^2 = r^2$ where r is the radius. With this system of equations, there can be two ordered pairs that intersect between the line and the circle. If there is one ordered pair, the line is tangent to the circle.

This system of equations is solved by substituting the expression mx in for y in the equation of a circle. Then, solve the equation for x. The values for x are substituted into the linear equation to find the value for y.

KEEP IN MIND

There will be two solutions in many cases with the system of a linear equation and an equation of a circle.

Example

Solve the system of equations, $\begin{matrix} y = -3x \\ x^2 + y^2 = 10 \end{matrix}$ **.**

A. $(1, 3)$ and $(-1, -3)$

B. $(1, -3)$ and $(-1, 3)$

C. $(-3, 10)$ and $(3, -10)$

D. $(3, 10)$ and $(-3, -10)$

The correct answer is **B.** The correct solutions are $(1, -3)$ and $(-1, 3)$.

$x^2 + (-3x)^2 = 10$	Substitute $-3x$ in for y in the second equation.
$x^2 + 9x^2 = 10$	Apply the exponent.
$10x^2 = 10$	Combine like terms on the left side of the equation.
$x^2 = 1$	Divide both sides of the equation by 10.
$x = \pm 1$	Apply the square root to both sides of the equation.
$y = -3(1) = -3$	Substitute 1 in the first equation and multiply.
$y = -3(-1) = 3$	Substitute -1 in the first equation and multiply.

Let's Review!

- There are three ways to solve a system of equations: graphing, substitution, and elimination. Using any method will result in the same solution for the system of equations.
- Solving a system of a linear equation and an equation of a circle uses substitution and usually results in two solutions.

INTERPRETING GRAPHICS

This lesson discusses how to create a bar, line, and circle graph and how to interpret data from these graphs. It also explores how to calculate and interpret the measures of central tendency.

Creating a Line, Bar, and Circle Graph

A line graph is a graph with points connected by segments that examines changes over time. The horizontal axis contains the independent variable (the input value), which is usually time. The vertical axis contains the dependent variable (the output value), which is an item that measures a quantity. A line graph will have a title and an appropriate scale to display the data. The graph can include more than one line.

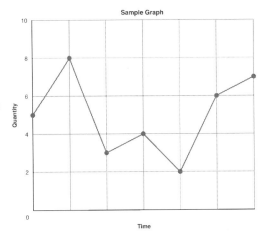

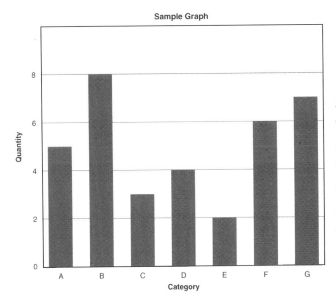

A bar graph uses rectangular horizontal or vertical bars to display information. A bar graph has categories on the horizontal axis and the quantity on the vertical axis. Bar graphs need a title and an appropriate scale for the frequency. The graph can include more than one bar.

BE CAREFUL

Make sure to use the appropriate scale for each type of graph.

A circle graph is a circular chart that is divided into parts, and each part shows the relative size of the value. To create a circle graph, find the total number and divide each part by the total to find the percentage. Then, to find the part of the circle, multiply each percent by 360°. Draw each part of the circle and create a title.

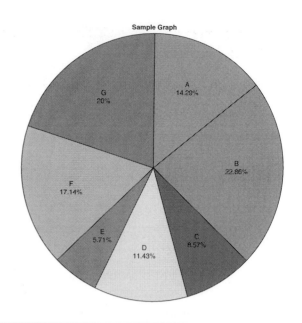

Examples

1. The table shows the amount of rainfall in inches. Select the line graph that represents this data.

Day	1	2	3	4	5	6	7	8	9	10	11	12
Rainfall Amount	0.5	0.2	0.4	1.1	1.6	0.9	0.7	1.3	1.5	0.8	0.5	0.1

A.
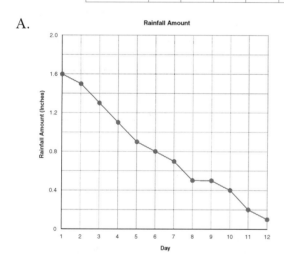

C.
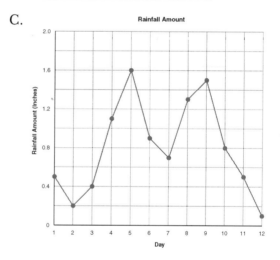

B.
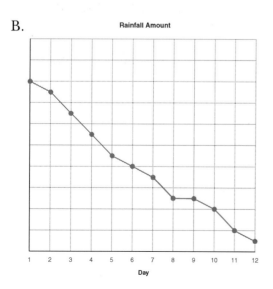

D.
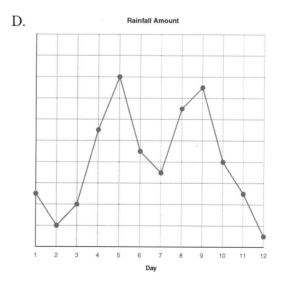

The correct answer is **C**. The graph is displayed correctly for the days with the appropriate labels.

2. **Students were surveyed about their favorite pet, and the table shows the results. Select the bar graph that represents this data.**

Pet	Quantity
Dog	14
Cat	16
Fish	4
Bird	8
Gerbil	7
Pig	3

A.

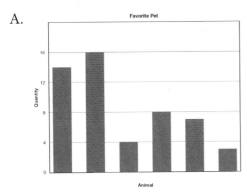

C.

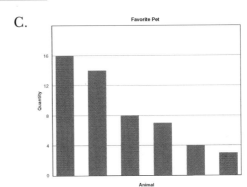

B.

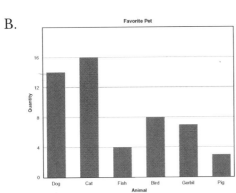

D.

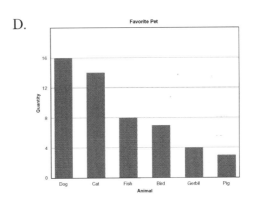

The correct answer is **B**. The bar graph represents each pet correctly and is labeled correctly.

3. The table shows the amount a family spends each month. Select the circle graph that represents the data.

Item	Food/Household Items	Bills	Mortgage	Savings	Miscellaneous
Amount	$700	$600	$400	$200	$100

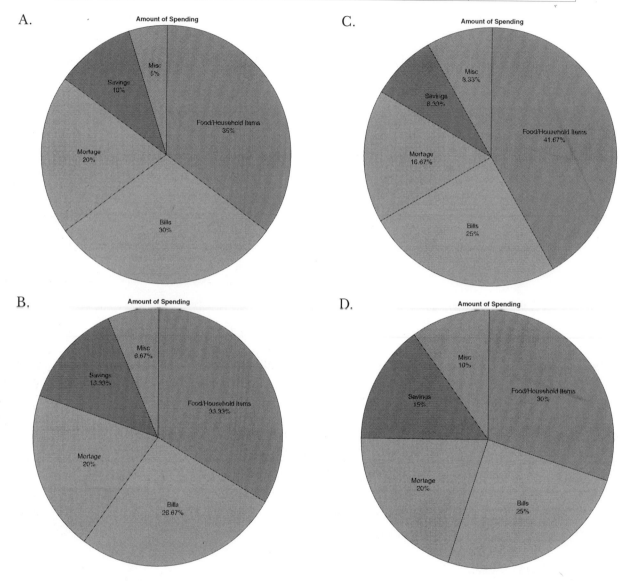

A.

B.

C.

D.

The correct answer is **A**. The total amount spent each month is $2,000. The section of the circle for food and household items is $\frac{700}{2,000} = 0.35 = 35\%$. The section of the circle for bills is $\frac{600}{2,000} = 0.30 = 30\%$. The section of the circle for mortgage is $\frac{400}{2,000} = 0.20 = 20\%$. The section of the circle for savings is $\frac{200}{2,000} = 0.10 = 10\%$. The section of the circle for miscellaneous is $\frac{100}{2,000} = 0.05 = 5\%$.

Interpreting and Evaluating Line, Bar, and Circle Graphs

Graph and charts are used to create visual examples of information, and it is important to be able to interpret them. The examples from Section 1 can show a variety of conclusions.

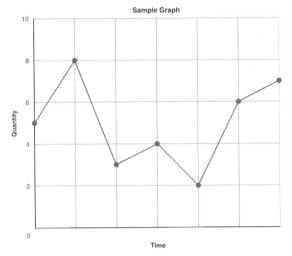

- The minimum value is 2, and the maximum value is 8.
- The largest decrease is between the second and third points.
- The largest increase is between the fifth and sixth points.

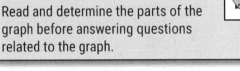

KEEP IN MIND

Read and determine the parts of the graph before answering questions related to the graph.

- Category B is the highest with 8.
- Category E is the lowest with 2.
- There are no categories that are the same.

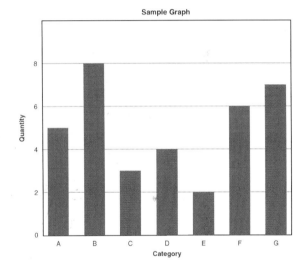

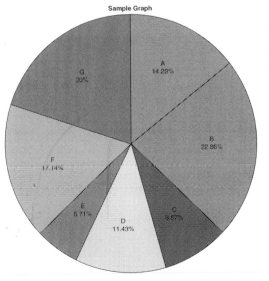

- Category B is the largest with 22.86%.
- Category E is the smallest with 5.71%.
- All of the categories are less than one-fourth of the graph.

55

Examples

1. The line chart shows the number of minutes a commuter drove to work during a month. Which statement is true for the line chart?

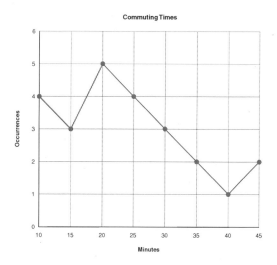

A. The commuter drove 25 minutes to work the most times

B. The commuter drove 25 minutes to work the fewest times.

C. The commuter took 10 minutes and 25 minutes twice during the month.

D. The commuter took 35 minutes and 45 minutes twice during the month.

The correct answer is **D**. The commuter took 35 minutes and 45 minutes twice during the month.

2. The bar chart shows the distance different families traveled for summer vacation. Which statement is true for the bar chart?

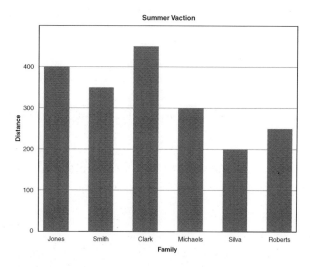

A. All families drove more than 200 miles.

B. The Clark family traveled 250 miles more than the Silva family.

C. The Roberts family traveled more miles than the Michaels family.

D. The Jones family is the only family that traveled 400 miles or more.

The correct answer is **B**. The correct solution is the Clark family traveled 250 miles more than the Silva family. The Clark family traveled 450 miles, and the Silva family traveled 200 miles, making the difference 250 miles.

3. Students were interviewed about their favorite subject in school. The circle graph shows the results. Which statement is true for the circle graph?

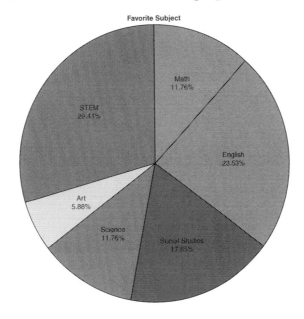

Favorite Subject

A. Math is the smallest percent for favorite subject.

B. The same number of students favor science and social studies.

C. English and STEM together are more than half of the respondents.

D. English and social students together are more than half of the respondents.

The correct answer is **C**. The correct solution is English and STEM together are more than half of the respondents because these values are more than 50% combined.

Mean, Median, Mode, and Range

The mean, median, mode, and range are common values related to data sets. These values can be calculated using the data set 2, 4, 7, 6, 8, 5, 6, and 3.

The mean is the sum of all numbers in a data set divided by the number of elements in the set. The sum of items in the data set is 41. Divide the value of 41 by the 8 items in the set. The mean is 5.125.

The median is the middle number of a data set when written in order. If there are an odd number of items, the median is the middle number. If there are an even number of items, the median is the mean of the middle two numbers. The

KEEP IN MIND

The mean, median, mode, and range can have the same values, depending on the data set.

numbers in order are 2, 3, 4, 5, 6, 6, 7, 8. The middle two numbers are 5 and 6. The mean of the two middle numbers is 5.5, which is the median.

The mode is the number or numbers that occur most often. There can be no modes, one mode, or many modes. In the data set, the number 6 appears twice, making 6 the mode.

The range is the difference between the highest and lowest values in a data set. The highest value is 8 and the lowest value is 2, for a range of 6.

Examples

1. Find the mean and the median for the data set 10, 20, 40, 20, 30, 50, 40, 60, 30, 10, 40, 20, 50, 70, and 80.

    A. The mean is 40, and the median is 38.

    B. The mean is 38, and the median is 40.

    C. The mean is 36, and the median is 50.

    D. The mean is 50, and the median is 36.

    The correct answer is **B**. The correct solution is the mean is 38 and the median is 40. The sum of all items is 570 divided by 15, which is 38. The data set in order is 10, 10, 20, 20, 20, 30, 30, 40, 40, 40, 50, 50, 60, 70, 80. The median number is 40.

2. Find the mode and the range for the data set 10, 20, 40, 20, 30, 50, 40, 60, 30, 10, 40, 20, 50, 70, and 80.

    A. The mode is 20, and the range is 70.

    B. The mode is 40, and the range is 70.

    C. The modes are 20 and 40, and the range is 70.

    D. The modes are 20, 40, and 70, and the range is 70.

    The correct answer is **C**. The correct solution is the modes are 20 and 40 and the range is 70. The modes are 20 and 40 because each of these numbers appears three times. The range is the difference between 80 and 10, which is 70.

Let's Review!

- A bar graph, line graph, and circle graph are different ways to summarize and represent data.
- The mean, median, mode, and range are values that can be used to interpret the meaning of a set of numbers.

POLYNOMIALS

This lesson introduces adding, subtracting, and multiplying polynomials. It also explains polynomial identities that describe numerical expressions.

Adding and Subtracting Polynomials

A **polynomial** is an expression that contains exponents, variables, constants, and operations. The exponents of the variables are only whole numbers, and there is no division by a variable. The operations are addition, subtraction,

KEEP IN MIND

The solution is an expression, and a value is not calculated for the variable.

multiplication, and division. Constants are terms without a variable. A polynomial of one term is a **monomial**; a polynomial of two terms is a **binomial**; and a polynomial of three terms is a **trinomial**.

To add polynomials, combine like terms and write the solution from the term with the highest exponent to the term with the lowest exponent. To simplify, first rearrange and group like terms. Next, combine like terms.

$(3x^2 + 5x–6) + (4x^3–3x + 4) = 4x^3 + 3x^2 + (5x–3x) + (–6 + 4) = 4x^3 + 3x^2 + 2x–2$

To subtract polynomials, rewrite the second polynomial using an additive inverse. Change the minus sign to a plus sign, and change the sign of every term inside the parentheses. Then, add the polynomials.

$(3x^2 + 5x–6)–(4x^3–3x + 4) = (3x^2 + 5x–6) + (–4x^3 + 3x–4) = –4x^3 + 3x^2 + (5x + 3x) + (–6–4)$

$= –4x^3 + 3x^2 + 8x–10$

Examples

1. **Perform the operation, $(2y^2–5y + 1) + (–3y^2 + 6y + 2)$.**

    A. $y^2 + y + 3$ B. $–y^2–y + 3$ C. $y^2–y + 3$ D. $–y^2 + y + 3$

    The correct answer is **D**. The correct solution is $–y^2 + y + 3$.

    $(2y^2–5y + 1) + (–3y^2 + 6y + 2) = (2y^2–3y^2) + (–5y + 6y) + (1 + 2) = –y^2 + y + 3$

2. **Perform the operation, $(3x^2y + 4xy–5xy^2)–(x^2y–3xy–2xy^2)$.**

    A. $2x^2y–7xy + 3xy^2$ C. $2x^2y + 7xy–3xy^2$

    B. $2x^2y + 7xy + 3xy^2$ D. $2x^2y–7xy–3xy^2$

    The correct answer is **C**. The correct solution is $2x^2y + 7xy–3xy^2$.

    $(3x^2y + 4xy–5xy^2)–(x^2y–3xy–2xy^2) = (3x^2y + 4xy–5xy^2) + (–x^2y + 3xy + 2xy^2)$
    $= (3x^2y–x^2y) + (4xy + 3xy) + (–5xy^2 + 2xy^2) = 2x^2y + 7xy–3xy^2$

Multiplying Polynomials

Multiplying polynomials comes in many forms. When multiplying a monomial by a monomial, multiply the coefficients and apply the multiplication rule for the power of an exponent.

BE CAREFUL!

Make sure that you apply the distributive property to all terms in the polynomials.

$$4xy(3x^2y) = 12x^3y^2.$$

When multiplying a monomial by a polynomial, multiply each term of the polynomial by the monomial.

$$4xy(3x^2y-2xy^2) = 4xy(3x^2y) + 4xy(-2xy^2) = 12x^3y^2-8x^2y^3.$$

When multiplying a binomial by a binomial, apply the distributive property and combine like terms.

$$(3x-4)(2x + 5) = 3x(2x + 5)-4(2x + 5) = 6x^2 + 15x-8x-20 = 6x^2 + 7x-20$$

When multiplying a binomial by a trinomial, apply the distributive property and combine like terms.

$$(x + 2)(3x^2-2x + 3) = (x + 2)(3x^2) + (x + 2)(-2x) + (x + 2)(3) = 3x^3 + 6x^2-2x^2-4x + 3x + 6 = 3x^3 + 4x^2-x + 6$$

Examples

1. **Multiply, $3xy^2(2x^2y)$.**

    A. $6x^2y^2$ B. $6x^3y^2$ C. $6x^3y^3$ D. $6x^2y^3$

    The correct answer is **C**. The correct solution is $6x^3y^3$. $3xy^2(2x^2y) = 6x^3y^3$.

2. **Multiply, $-2xy(3xy-4x^2y^2)$.**

    A. $-6x^2y^2 + 8x^3y^3$ B. $-6x^2y^2-8x^3y^3$ C. $-6xy + 8x^3y^3$ D. $-6xy-8x^3y^3$

    The correct answer is **A**. The correct solution is $-6x^2y^2 + 8x^3y^3$.

    $$-2xy(3xy-4x^2y^2) = -2xy(3xy)-2xy(-4x^2y^2) = -6x^2y^2 + 8x^3y^3$$

Polynomial Identities

BE CAREFUL!

Pay attention to the details of each polynomial identity and apply them appropriately.

There are many polynomial identities that show relationships between expressions.

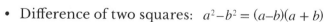

- Difference of two squares: $a^2-b^2 = (a-b)(a + b)$
- Square of a binomial: $(a + b)^2 = a^2 + ab + b^2$
- Square of a binomial: $(a-b)^2 = a^2-ab + b^2$
- Sum of cubes: $a^3 + b^3 = (a + b)(a^2-ab + b^2)$
- Difference of two cubes: $a^3-b^3 = (a-b)(a^2 + ab + b^2)$

Examples

1. **Apply the polynomial identity to rewrite $x^2 + 6x + 9$.**

    A. $x^2 + 9$ B. $(x^2 + 3)^2$ C. $(x + 3)^2$ D. $(3x)^2$

    The correct answer is **C**. The correct solution is $(x + 3)^2$. The expression $x^2 + 6x + 9$ is rewritten as $(x + 3)^2$ because the value of a is x and the value of b is 3.

2. **Apply the polynomial identity to rewrite $8x^3 - 1$.**

    A. $(2x + 1)(4x^2 + 2x - 1)$ C. $(2x + 1)(4x^2 - 2x + 1)$

    B. $(2x - 1)(4x^2 - 2x - 1)$ D. $(2x - 1)(4x^2 + 2x + 1)$

    The correct answer is **D**. The correct solution is $(2x - 1)(4x^2 + 2x + 1)$. The expression $8x^3 - 1$ is rewritten as $(2x - 1)(4x^2 + 2x + 1)$ because the value of a is $2x$ and the value of b is 1.

Let's Review!

- Adding, subtracting, and multiplying are commonly applied to polynomials. The key step in applying these operations is combining like terms.
- Polynomial identities require rewriting polynomials into different forms.

POWERS, EXPONENTS, ROOTS, AND RADICALS

This lesson introduces how to apply the properties of exponents and examines square roots and cube roots. It also discusses how to estimate quantities using integer powers of 10.

Properties of Exponents

An expression that is a repeated multiplication of the same factor is a **power**. The **exponent** is the number of times the **base** is multiplied. For example, 6^2 is the same as 6 times 6, or 36. There are many rules associated with exponents.

Property	Definition	Examples
Product Rule (Same Base)	$a^m \times a^n = a^{m+n}$	$4^1 \times 4^4 = 4^{1+4} = 4^5 = 1024$ $x^1 \times x^4 = x^{1+4} = x^5$
Product Rule (Different Base)	$a^m \times b^m = (a \times b)^m$	$2^2 \times 3^2 = (2 \times 3)^2 = 6^2 = 36$ $3^3 \times x^3 = (3 \times x)^3 = (3x)^3 = 27x^3$
Quotient Rule (Same Base)	$\dfrac{a^m}{a^n} = a^{m-n}$	$\dfrac{4^4}{4^2} = 4^{4-2} = 4^2 = 16$ $\dfrac{x^6}{x^3} = x^{6-3} = x^3$
Quotient Rule (Different Base)	$\dfrac{a^m}{b^m} = \left(\dfrac{a}{b}\right)^m$	$\dfrac{4^4}{3^4} = \left(\dfrac{4}{3}\right)^4$ $\dfrac{x^6}{y^6} = \left(\dfrac{x}{y}\right)^6$
Power of a Power Rule	$(a^m)^n = a^{mn}$	$(2^2)^3 = 2^{2\times3} = 2^6 = 64$ $(x^5)^8 = x^{5\times8} = x^{40}$
Zero Exponent Rule	$a^0 = 1$	$64^0 = 1$ $y^0 = 1$
Negative Exponent Rule	$a^{-m} = \dfrac{1}{a^m}$	$3^{-3} = \dfrac{1}{3^3} = \dfrac{1}{27}$ $\dfrac{1}{x^{-3}} = x^3$

For many exponent expressions, it is necessary to use multiplication rules to simplify the expression completely.

Examples

1. **Simplify $(3^2)^3$.**

   A. 18   C. 243

   B. 216   D. 729

   The correct answer is **D**. The correct solution is 729 because $(3^2)^3 = 3^{2\times3} = 3^6 = 729$.

> **KEEP IN MIND**
>
> The expressions
> $(-2)^2 = (-2) \times (-2) = 4$ and
> $-2^2 = -(2 \times 2) = -4$ have different results because of the location of the negative signs and parentheses. For each problem, focus on each detail to simplify completely and correctly.

2. **Simplify $(2x^2)^4$.**

   A. $2x^8$ B. $4x^4$ C. $8x^6$ D. $16x^8$

   The correct answer is **D**. The correct solution is $16x^8$ because $(2x^2)^4 = 2^4(x^2)^4 = 2^4 x^{2\times4} = 16x^8$.

3. Simplify $\left(\frac{x^{-2}}{y^2}\right)^3$.

A. $\frac{1}{x^6 y^6}$ B. $\frac{x^6}{y^6}$ C. $\frac{y^6}{x^6}$ D. $x^6 y^6$

The correct answer is **A**. The correct solution is $\frac{1}{x^6 y^6}$ because $\left(\frac{x^{-2}}{y^2}\right)^3 = \left(\frac{1}{x^2 y^2}\right)^3 = \frac{1}{x^{2\times3} y^{2\times3}} = \frac{1}{x^6 y^6}$.

Square Root and Cube Roots

The **square** of a number is the number raised to the power of 2. The **square root** of a number, when the number is squared, gives that number. $10^2 = 100$, so the square of 100 is 10, or $\sqrt{100} = 10$. **Perfect squares** are numbers with whole number square roots, such as 1, 4, 9, 16, and 25.

Squaring a number and taking a square root are opposite operations, meaning that the operations undo each other. This means that $\sqrt{x^2} = x$ and $(\sqrt{x})^2 = x$. When solving the equation $x^2 = p$, the solutions are $x = \pm\sqrt{p}$ because a negative value squared is a positive solution.

The **cube** of a number is the number raised to the power of 3. The **cube root** of a number, when the number is cubed, gives that number. $10^3 = 1000$, so the cube of 1,000 is 100, or $\sqrt[3]{1000} = 10$. **Perfect cubes** are numbers with whole number cube roots, such as 1, 8, 27, 64, and 125.

KEEP IN MIND

Most square roots and cube roots are not perfect roots.

Cubing a number and taking a cube root are opposite operations, meaning that the operations undo each other. This means that $\sqrt[3]{x^3} = x$ and $\left(\sqrt[3]{x}\right)^3 = x$. When solving the equation $x^3 = p$, the solution is $x = \sqrt[3]{p}$.

If a number is not a perfect square root or cube root, the solution is an approximation. When this occurs, the solution is an irrational number. For example, $\sqrt{2}$ is the irrational solution to $x^2 = 2$.

Examples

1. Solve $x^2 = 121$.

A. $-10, 10$ B. $-11, 11$ C. $-12, 12$ D. $-13, 13$

The correct answer is **B**. The correct solution is $-11, 11$ because the square root of 121 is 11. The values of -11 and 11 make the equation true.

2. Solve $x^3 = 125$.

A. 1 B. 5 C. 10 D. 25

The correct answer is **B**. The correct solution is 5 because the cube root of 125 is 5.

Express Large or Small Quantities as Multiples of 10

Scientific notation is a large or small number written in two parts. The first part is a number between 1 and 10. In these problems, the first digit will be a single digit. The number is followed by a multiple to a power of 10. A positive integer exponent means the number is greater than 1, while a negative integer exponent means the number is smaller than 1.

> **KEEP IN MIND**
>
> A positive exponent in scientific notation represents a large number, while a negative exponent represents a small number.

The number 3×10^4 is the same as $3 \times 10,000 = 30,000$.

The number 3×10^{-4} is the same as $3 \times 0.0001 = 0.0003$.

For example, the population of the United States is about 3×10^8, and the population of the world is about 7×10^9. The population of the United States is 300,000,000, and the population of the world is 7,000,000,000. The world population is about 20 times larger than the population of the United States.

Examples

1. **The population of China is about 1×10^9, and the population of the United States is about 3×10^8. How many times larger is the population of China than the population of the United States?**

    A. 2   B. 3   C. 4   D. 5

    The correct answer is **B**. The correct solution is 3 because the population of China is about 1,000,000,000 and the population of the United States is about 300,000,000. So the population is about 3 times larger.

2. **A red blood cell has a length of 8×10^{-6} meter, and a skin cell has a length of 3×10^{-5} meter. How many times larger is the skin cell?**

    A. 1   B. 2   C. 3   D. 4

    The correct answer is **D**. The correct solution is 4 because 3×10^{-5} is 0.00003 and 8×10^{-6} is 0.000008. So, the skin cell is about 4 times larger.

Let's Review!

- The properties and rules of exponents are applicable to generate equivalent expressions.
- Only a few whole numbers out of the set of whole numbers are perfect squares. Perfect cubes can be positive or negative.
- Numbers expressed in scientific notation are useful to compare large or small numbers.

STATISTICS & PROBABILITY: THE RULES OF PROBABILITY

This lesson explores a sample space and its outcomes and provides an introduction to probability, including how to calculate expected values and analyze decisions based on probability.

Sample Space

A **sample space** is the set of all possible outcomes. Using a deck of cards labeled 1–10, the sample space is 1, 2, 3, 4, 5, 6, 7, 8, 9, and 10. An **event** is a subset of the sample space. For example, if a card is drawn and the outcome of the event is an even number, possible results are 2, 4, 6, 8, 10.

The **union** of two events is everything in both events, and the notation is $A \cup B$. The union of events is associated with the word *or*. For example, a card is drawn that is either a multiple of 3 or a multiple of 4. The set containing the multiples of 3 is 3, 6, and 9. The set containing the multiples of 4 is 4 and 8. The union of the set is 3, 4, 6, 8, and 9.

> **KEEP IN MIND**
>
> The intersection of an event can have no values. The intersection of drawing a card that is even and odd is a set with no values because a card cannot be both even and odd. The complement of an event is the "not," or the opposite of, the event.

The **intersection** of two events is all of the events in both sets, and the notation is $A \cap B$. The intersection of events is associated with the word *and*. For example, a card is drawn that is even and a multiple of 4. The set containing even numbers is 2, 4, 6, 8, and 10. The set containing the multiples of 4 is 4 and 8. The intersection is 4 and 8 because these numbers are in both sets.

The **complement** of an event is an outcome that is not part of the set. The complement of an event is associated with the word *not*. A card is drawn and is not a multiple of 5. The set not containing multiples of 5 is 1, 2, 3, 4, 6, 7, 8, and 9. The complement of not a multiple of 5 is 1, 2, 3, 4, 6, 7, 8, and 9.

Examples

Use the following table of the results when rolling two six-sided number cubes.

1, 1	1, 2	1, 3	1, 4	1, 5	1, 6
2, 1	2, 2	2, 3	2, 4	2, 5	2, 6
3, 1	3, 2	3, 3	3, 4	3, 5	3, 6
4, 1	4, 2	4, 3	4, 4	4, 5	4, 6
5, 1	5, 2	5, 3	5, 4	5, 5	5, 6
6, 1	6, 2	6, 3	6, 4	6, 5	6, 6

1. **How many possible outcomes are there for the union of rolling a sum of 3 or a sum of 5?**

   A. 2   B. 4   C. 6   D. 8

   The correct answer is **C**. The correct solution is 6 possible outcomes. There are two options for the first event (2, 1) and (1, 2). There are 4 options for the second event (4, 1), (3, 2), (2, 3), and (1, 4). The union of two events is six possible outcomes.

2. **How many possible outcomes are there for the intersection of rolling a double and a multiple of 3?**

   A. 0   B. 2   C. 4   D. 6

   The correct answer is **B**. The correct solution is 2 possible outcomes. There are six options for the first event (1, 1), (2, 2), (3, 3), (4, 4), (5, 5), and (6, 6). There are 12 options for the second event of the multiple of three. The intersection is (3, 3) and (6, 6) because these numbers meet both requirements.

3. **How many possible outcomes are there for the complement of rolling a 3 and a 5?**

   A. 16   B. 18   C. 27   D. 36

   The correct answer is **A**. The correct solution is 16 possible outcomes. There are 16 options of not rolling a 3 or a 5.

Probability

The **probability** of an event is the number of favorable outcomes divided by the total number of possible outcomes.

$$Probability = \frac{number\ of\ favorable\ outcomes}{number\ of\ possible\ outcomes}$$

Probability is a value between 0 (event does not happen) and 1 (event will happen). For example, the probability of getting heads when a coin is flipped is $\frac{1}{2}$ because heads is 1 option out of 2 possibilities.

BE CAREFUL!

Make sure that you apply the correct formula for the probability of an event.

The probability of rolling an odd number on a six-sided number cube is $\frac{3}{6} = \frac{1}{2}$ because there are three odd numbers, 1, 3, and 5, out of 6 possible numbers.

The probability of an "or" event happening is the sum of the events happening. For example, the probability of rolling an odd number or a 4 on a six-sided number cube is $\frac{4}{6}$. The probability of rolling an odd number is $\frac{3}{6}$, and the probability of rolling a 4 is $\frac{1}{6}$. Therefore, the probability is $\frac{3}{6} + \frac{1}{6} = \frac{4}{6} = \frac{2}{3}$.

The probability of an "and" event happening is the product of the probability of two or more events. The probability of rolling 6 three times in a row is $\frac{1}{216}$. The probability of a single event is $\frac{1}{6}$, and this fraction is multiplied three times to find the probability, $\frac{1}{6} \times \frac{1}{6} \times \frac{1}{6}$. There are cases of "with replacement" when the item is returned to the pile and "without replacement" when the item is not returned to the pile.

The probability of a "not" event happening is 1 minus the probability of the event occurring. For example, the probability of not rolling 6 three times in a row is $1-\frac{1}{216}=\frac{215}{216}$.

Examples

1. **A deck of cards contains 40 cards divided into 4 colors: red, blue, green, and yellow. Each group has cards numbered 0–9. What is the probability of selecting an 8?**

   A. $\frac{1}{10}$ B. $\frac{1}{8}$ C. $\frac{1}{4}$ D. $\frac{1}{2}$

   The correct answer is **A**. The correct solution is $\frac{1}{10}$. There are 4 cards out of 40 that contain the number 8, making the probability $\frac{4}{40}=\frac{1}{10}$.

2. **A deck of cards contains 40 cards divided into 4 colors: red, blue, green, and yellow. Each group has cards numbered 0–9. What is the probability of selecting an even or a red card?**

   A. $\frac{1}{4}$ B. $\frac{3}{8}$ C. $\frac{5}{8}$ D. $\frac{3}{4}$

   The correct answer is **C**. The correct solution is $\frac{5}{8}$. There are 20 even cards and 10 red cards. The overlap of 5 red even cards is subtracted from the probability, $\frac{20}{40}+\frac{10}{40}-\frac{5}{40}=\frac{25}{40}=\frac{5}{8}$.

3. **A deck of cards contains 40 cards divided into 4 colors: red, blue, green, and yellow. Each group has cards numbered 0–9. What is the probability of selecting a blue card first, replacing the card, and selecting a 9?**

   A. $\frac{1}{100}$ B. $\frac{1}{80}$ C. $\frac{1}{40}$ D. $\frac{1}{20}$

   The correct answer is **C**. The correct solution is $\frac{1}{40}$. There are 10 blue cards and 4 cards that contain the number 9. The probability of the event is $\frac{10}{40}\times\frac{4}{40}=\frac{40}{1600}=\frac{1}{40}$.

4. **A deck of cards contains 40 cards divided into 4 colors: red, blue, green, and yellow. Each group has cards numbered 0–9. What is the probability of NOT selecting a green card?**

   A. $\frac{1}{4}$ B. $\frac{3}{8}$ C. $\frac{1}{2}$ D. $\frac{3}{4}$

   The correct answer is **D**. The correct solution is $\frac{3}{4}$. There are 10 cards that are green, making the probability of NOT selecting a green card $1-\frac{10}{40}=\frac{30}{40}=\frac{3}{4}$.

Calculating Expected Values and Analyzing Decisions Based on Probability

The **expected value** of an event is the sum of the products of the probability of an event times the payoff of an event. A good example is calculating the expected value for buying a lottery ticket. There is a one in a hundred million chance that a person would win $50 million. Each ticket costs $2. The expected value is

$$\frac{1}{100,000,000}(50,000,000-2)+\frac{99,999,999}{100,000,000}(-2)=\frac{49,999,998}{100,000,000}-\frac{199,999,998}{100,000,000}=-\frac{150,000,000}{100,000,000}--\$1.50$$

On average, one should expect to lose $1.50 each time the game is played. Analyzing the

BE CAREFUL!

The expected value will not be the same as the actual value unless the probability of winning is 100%.

information, the meaning of the data shows that playing the lottery would result in losing money every time.

Examples

1. What is the expected value of an investment if the probability is $\frac{1}{5}$ of losing $1,000, $\frac{1}{4}$ of no gain, $\frac{2}{5}$ of making $1,000, and $\frac{3}{20}$ of making $2,000?

   A. $0 B. $200 C. $500 D. $700

   The correct answer is **C**. The correct solution is 500. The expected value is $\frac{1}{5}(-1,000) + \frac{1}{4}(0) + \frac{2}{5}(1,000) + \frac{3}{20}(2,000) = -200 + 0 + 400 + 300 = \$500$.

2. The table below shows the value of the prizes and the probability of winning a prize in a contest.

Prize	$10	$100	$5,000	$50,000
Probability	1 in 50	1 in 1,000	1 in 50,000	1 in 250,000

   Calculate the expected value.

   A. $0.10 B. $0.20 C. $0.50 D. $0.60

   The correct answer is **D**. The correct solution is $0.60. The probability for each event is

Prize	$10	$100	$5,000	$50,000	Not Winning
Probability	1 in 50 = 0.02	1 in 1,000 = 0.001	1 in 50,000 = 0.00002	1 in 250,000 = 0.000004	0.978976

   The expected value is $0.02(10) + 0.001(100) + 0.00002(5,000) + 0.000004(50,000) + 0.978976(0) = 0.2 + 0.1 + 0.1 + 0.2 + 0 = \$0.60$.

3. Which option results in the largest loss on a product?

   A. 40% of gaining $100,000 and 60% of losing $100,000
   B. 60% of gaining $250,000 and 40% of losing $500,000
   C. 30% of gaining $400,000 and 70% of losing $250,000
   D. 60% of gaining $250,000 and 40% of losing $450,000

   The correct answer is **C**. The correct solution is 30% of gaining $400,000 and 70% of losing $250,000. The expected value is $0.30(400,000) + 0.7(-250,000) = 120,000 + (-175,000) = -55,000$.

Let's Review!

- The sample space is the number of outcomes of an event. The union, the intersection, and the complement are related to the sample space.
- The probability of an event is the number of possible events divided by the total number of outcomes. There can be "and," "or," and "not" probabilities.
- The expected value of an event is based on the payout and probability of an event occurring.

STATISTICAL MEASURES

This lesson explores the different sampling techniques using random and non-random sampling. The lesson also distinguishes among different study techniques. In addition, it provides simulations that compare results with expected outcomes.

Probability and Non-Probability Sampling

A population includes all items within a set of data, while a sample consists of one or more observations from a population.

The collection of data samples from a population is an important part of research and helps researcher draw conclusions related to populations. Probability sampling creates a sample from a population by using random sampling techniques.

KEEP IN MIND
Probability sampling is random, and non-probability sampling is not random.

Every person within a population has an equal chance of being selected for a sample. Non-probability sampling creates a sample from a population without using random sampling techniques.

There are four types of probability sampling. Simple random sampling is assigning a number to each member of a population and randomly selecting numbers. Stratified sampling uses simple random sampling after the population is split into equal groups. Systematic sampling chooses every n^{th} member from a list or a group. Cluster random sampling uses natural groups in a population: the population is divided into groups, and random samples are collected from groups.

Each type of probability sampling has an advantage and a disadvantage when finding an appropriate sample.

Probability Sampling	Advantage	Disadvantage
Simple random sampling	Most cases have a sample representative of a population	Not efficient for large samples
Stratified random sampling	Creates layers of random samples from different groups representative of a population	Not efficient for large samples
Systematic sampling	Creates a sample representative of population without a random number selection	Not as random as simple random sampling
Cluster random sampling	Relatively easy and convenient to implement	Might not work if clusters are different from one another

There are four types of non-probability sampling. Convenience sampling produces samples that are easy to access. Volunteer sampling asks for volunteers or recommendations for a sample. Purposive sampling bases samples on specific characteristics by selecting samples from a group that meets the qualifications of the study. Quota sampling is choosing samples of groups of the subpopulation.

Examples

1. **A factory is studying the quality of beverage samples. There are 50 bottles randomly chosen from one shipment every 60 minutes. What type of sampling is used?**

    A. Systematic sampling
    B. Simple random sampling
    C. Cluster random sampling
    D. Stratified random sampling

    The correct answer is **C**. The correct solution is cluster random sampling because bottles of beverage are selected within specific boundaries.

2. **A group conducting a survey asks a person for his or her opinion. Then, the group asks the person being surveyed for the names of 10 friends to obtain additional options. What type of sampling is used?**

    A. Quota sampling
    B. Volunteer sampling
    C. Purposive sampling
    D. Convenience sampling

    The correct answer is **B**. The correct solution is volunteer sampling because the group is looking for recommendations.

Census, Surveys, Experiments, Observational Studies

Various sampling techniques are used to collect data from a population. These are in the form of a census, a survey, observational studies, or experiments.

A census collects data by asking everyone in a population the same question. Asking everyone at school or everyone at work are examples of a

> **KEEP IN MIND**
>
> A census includes everyone within a population, and a survey includes every subject of a sample. An observational study involves watching groups randomly, and an experiment involves assigning groups.

census. A survey collects data on every subject within a sample. The subjects can be determined by convenience sampling or by simple random sampling. Examples of surveys are asking sophomores at school or first shift workers at work.

In an observational study, data collection occurs by watching or observing an event. Watching children who play outside and observing if they drink water or sports drinks is an example. An experiment is way of finding information by assigning people to groups and collecting data on observations. Assigning one group of children to drink water and another group to drink sports drinks after playing and making comparisons is an example of an experiment.

Examples

1. **A school wants to create a census to identify students' favorite subject in school. Which group should the school ask?**

   A. All staff

   B. All students

   C. All sophomores

   D. All male students

   The correct answer is **B**. The correct solution is all students because this gathers information on the entire population.

2. **A researcher records the arrival time of employees at a job based on their actual start time. What type of study is this?**

   A. Census

   B. Survey

   C. Experiment

   D. Observational study

   The correct answer is **D**. The correct solution is observational study because the researcher is observing the time the employees arrive at work.

3. **The local county wants to test the water quality of a stream by collecting samples. What should the county collect?**

   A. The water quality at one spot

   B. The water quality under trees

   C. The water quality under bridges

   D. The water quality at different spots

   The correct answer is **D**. The correct solution is the water quality at different spots because this survey allows for the collection of different samples.

Simulations

A simulation enables researchers to study real-world events by modeling events. Advantages of simulations are that they are quick, easy, and inexpensive; the disadvantage is that the results are approximations. The steps to complete a simulation are as follows:

KEEP IN MIND

A simulation is only useful if the results closely mirror real-world outcomes.

- Describe the outcomes.
- Assign a random value to the outcomes.
- Choose a source to generate the outcomes.
- Generate values for the outcomes until a consistent pattern emerges.
- Analyze the results.

Examples

1. **A family has two children and wants to simulate the gender of the children. Which object would be beneficial to use for the simulation?**

   A. Coin

   B. Four-section spinner

   C. Six-sided number cube

   D. Random number generator

   The correct answer is **B**. The correct solution is a four-section spinner because there are four possible outcomes of the event (boy/boy, boy/girl, girl/boy, and girl/girl).

2. **There are six options from which to choose a meal at a festival. A model using a six-sided number cube is used to represent the simulation.**

Hamburger	Chicken	Hot Dog	Bratwurst	Pork Chop	Fish	Total
1	2	3	4	5	6	
83	82	85	89	86	75	500

   Choose the statement that correctly answers whether the simulation of using a six-sided number cube is consistent with the actual number of dinners sold and then explains why or why not.

   A. The simulation is consistent because it has six equally likely outcomes.

   B. The simulation is consistent because it has two equally likely outcomes.

   C. The simulation is not consistent because of the limited number of outcomes.

   D. The simulation is not consistent because of the unlimited number of outcomes.

   The correct answer is **A**. The correct solution is the simulation is consistent because it has six equally likely outcomes. The six-sided number cube provides consistent outcomes because there is an equal opportunity to select any dinner.

Let's Review!

- Probability (random) sampling and non-probability (not random) sampling are ways to collect data.
- Censuses, surveys, experiments, and observational studies are ways to collect data from a population.
- A simulation is way to model random events and compare the results to real-world outcomes.

CHAPTER 2 ALGEBRA PRACTICE QUIZ 1

1. Solve the equation for the unknown,
    $3(x + 4)-1 = 2(x + 3)-2$.

    A. −7

    B. −2

    C. 2

    D. 7

2. Solve the equation for the unknown,
    $4x + 3 = 8$.

    A. −2

    B. $-\frac{5}{4}$

    C. $\frac{5}{4}$

    D. 2

3. Solve the system of equations by
    graphing, $\begin{matrix} y = 4x-3 \\ y = x \end{matrix}$.

    A.

    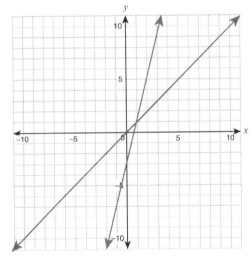

    B.

    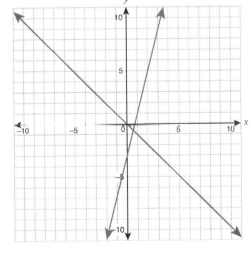

    C.

    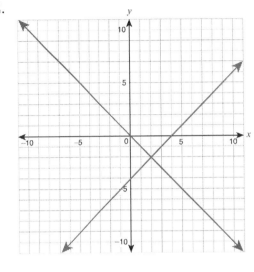

    D.

    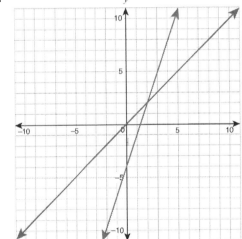

4. Solve the system of equations,
    $2x-3y = -1$
    $x + 2y = 24$.

    A. (7, 10)

    B. (10, 7)

    C. (6, 8)

    D. (8, 6)

5. The table shows the temperature in Fahrenheit degrees for two cities the first ten days of December. Select the correct line graph for this data.

Day	1	2	3	4	5	6	7	8	9	10
City 1	25	18	34	29	32	26	19	15	12	7
City 2	14	20	22	18	20	18	14	9	8	11

A.

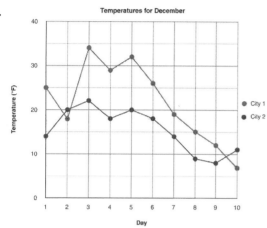

C.

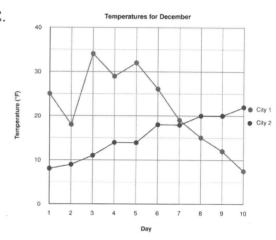

B.

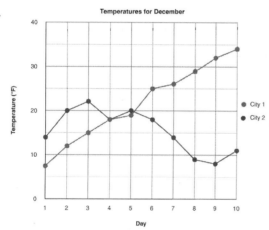

D.

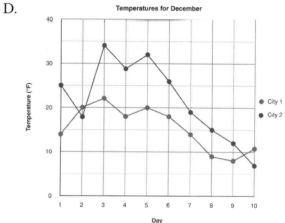

6. **Elementary school students were surveyed about their favorite animals at a zoo. The circle graph shows the results. Which statement is true for the circle graph?**

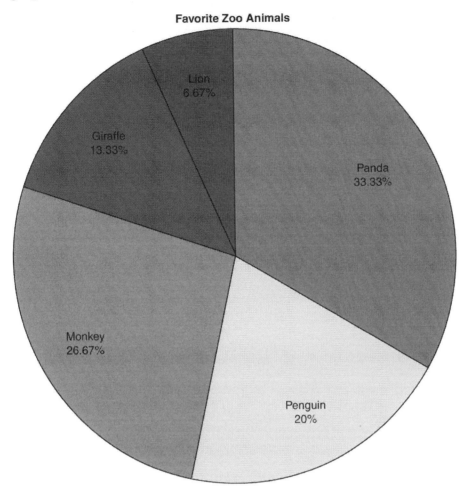

Favorite Zoo Animals

Lion 6.67%

Giraffe 13.33%

Panda 33.33%

Monkey 26.67%

Penguin 20%

A. The penguins were the second-favorite animals.

B. No group of animals makes up one-third of the graph.

C. Sixty percent of the students like pandas and monkeys.

D. Fifty percent of the students like giraffes, lions, and penguins.

7. Multiply, $(x-1)(x^2 + 2x + 3)$.

   A. $x^3 + x^2 + x-3$ C. $x^3 + x^2-x-3$

   B. x^3-x^2-x-3 D. $x^3-x^2 + x-3$

8. Multiply, $(3x^2-2)(x-3)$.

   A. $3x^3 + 9x^2-2x + 6$

   B. $3x^3-9x^2-2x + 6$

   C. $3x^3 + 9x^2-2x-6$

   D. $3x^3-9x^2-2x-6$

9. A lysosome has a length of 1×10^{-6} meter, and measles virus has a length of 2×10^{-9} meter. How many times longer is the lysosome?

   A. 5   C. 500

   B. 50   D. 5,000

10. Solve $x^3 = 343$.

   A. 6   C. 8

   B. 7   D. 9

11. There are 4,000 students at a high school. A simulation was completed for 50 students indicating that 35 intend to go to college. How can this simulation improve to provide a more accurate outcome?

   A. Simulate 100 students in each grade.

   B. Simulate 1,000 students in the school.

   C. Run multiple simulations of 50 students.

   D. Run multiple simulations of 100 students.

12. A survey group wants to know the percentage of voters in a town who favor building a new shopping center. What is the survey group's population?

   A. All eligible voters in the town

   B. All people who live in the town

   C. All interviewed people in the town

   D. All voters 35 years and older in the town

13. A life insurance policy has an annual premium of $600. In case of death, the insurance company will pay $500,000. The probability of dying is 0.0015. What is the expected value after one year?

   A. –$750   C. $150

   B. –$150   D. $750

14. In a deck of 20 number cards, cards 1–5 are green, cards 6–10 are red, cards 11–15 are yellow, and cards 16–20 are blue. Describe the intersection of an odd number and blue cards.

   A. Cards 17 and 19

   B. Cards 16, 17, 18, 19, and 20

   C. Cards 11, 13, 15, 17, and 19

   D. Cards 1, 3, 5, 7, 9, 11, 13, 15, 17, and 19

CHAPTER 2 ALGEBRA
PRACTICE QUIZ 1 — ANSWER KEY

1. **A.** The correct solution is –7.

$3x + 12{-}1 = 2x + 6{-}2$	Apply the distributive property.
$3x + 11 = 2x + 4$	Combine like terms on both sides of the equation.
$x + 11 = 4$	Subtract $2x$ from both sides of the equation.
$x = -7$	Subtract 11 from both sides of the equation.

See Lesson: Equations with One Variable.

2. **C.** The correct solution is $\frac{5}{4}$.

$4x = 5$	Subtract 3 from both sides of the equation.
$x = \frac{5}{4}$	Divide both sides of the equation by 4.

See Lesson: Equations with One Variable.

3. **A.** The correct graph has the two lines intersect at (1, 1). **See Lesson: Equations with Two Variables.**

4. **B.** The correct solution is (10, 7).

$-2x{-}4y = -48$	Multiply all terms in the second equation by -2.
$-7y = -49$	Add the equations.
$y = 7$	Divide both sides of the equation by -7.
$x + 2(7) = 24$	Substitute 7 in the second equation for y.
$x + 14 = 24$	Simplify using order of operations.
$x = 10$	Subtract 14 from both sides of the equation.

See Lesson: Equations with Two Variables.

5. **A.** The correct solution is A because the points for each city are graphed correctly. **See Lesson: Interpreting Graphics.**

6. **C.** The correct solution is that 60 percent of the students like pandas and monkeys: 33.33% plus 26.67% equals 60%. **See Lesson: Interpreting Graphics.**

7. **A.** The correct solution is $x^3 + x^2 + x{-}3$.

$$(x{-}1)(x^2 + 2x + 3) = (x{-}1)(x^2) + (x{-}1)(2x) + (x{-}1)(3) = x^3{-}x^2 + 2x^2{-}2x + 3x{-}3 = x^3 + x^2 + x{-}3$$

See Lesson: Polynomials.

8. B. The correct solution is $3x^3 - 9x^2 - 2x + 6$.

$$(3x^2 - 2)(x-3) = 3x^2(x-3) - 2(x-3) = 3x^3 - 9x^2 - 2x + 6$$

See Lesson: Polynomials.

9. A. The correct solution is 500 because 1×10^{-6} is 0.000001 and 2×10^{-9} is about 0.000000002. So, the lysosome is 500 times longer. **See Lesson: Powers, Exponents, Roots, and Radicals.**

10. B. The correct solution is 7 because the cube root of 343 is 7. **See Lesson: Powers, Exponents, Roots, and Radicals.**

11. B. The correct solution is simulating 1,000 students in the school because this would provide more accurate results representing students' intentions. **See Lesson: Statistical Measures.**

12. A. The correct solution is all eligible voters in the town because this is the population for the entire survey. **See Lesson: Statistical Measures**

13. C. The correct solution is $150. The expected value is $0.0015(499,400) + 0.9985(-600)$ $= 749.1 + (-599.1) = \$150$. **See Lesson: Statistics & Probability: The Rules of Probability.**

14. A. The correct solution is cards 17 and 19. Odd number cards are 1, 3, 5, 7, 9, 11, 13, 15, 17, and 19. Blue cards are 16, 17, 18, 19, and 20. Cards 17 and 19 are the only two cards that are blue and odd numbers. **See Lesson: Statistics & Probability: The Rules of Probability.**

CHAPTER 2 ALGEBRA PRACTICE QUIZ 2

1. Solve the equation for the unknown, $\frac{x}{2} + 5 = 8$.

   A. $\frac{3}{2}$ C. 6

   B. $\frac{5}{2}$ D. 26

2. Solve the equation for the unknown, $3x - 8 + 5 + 2x = 4x - x + 6$.

   A. $-\frac{9}{2}$ C. $\frac{2}{9}$

   B. $-\frac{2}{9}$ D. $\frac{9}{2}$

3. Solve the system of equations,
   $-2x + 2y = 28$
   $3x + y = -22$.

   A. $(9, 5)$ C. $(9, -5)$

   B. $(-9, -5)$ D. $(-9, 5)$

4. Solve the system of equations by graphing,
   $y = \frac{1}{3}x + 2$
   $y = \frac{2}{3}x + 5$.

   A.

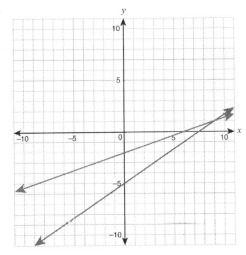

B.

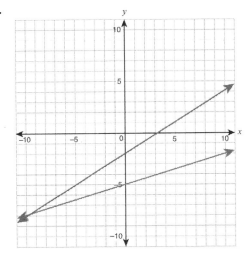

C.

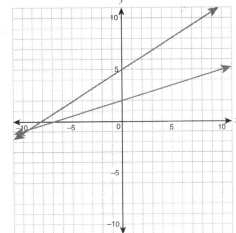

D.

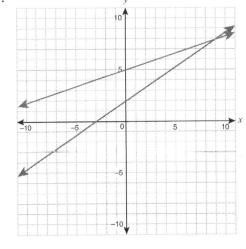

5. The table shows the number of students in grades kindergarten through sixth grade. Select the correct bar graph for this data.

Grade	Kindergarten	1st	2nd	3rd	4th	5th	6th
Number of Students	135	150	140	155	145	165	170

A.

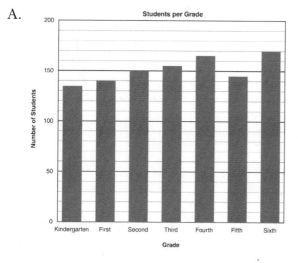

C.

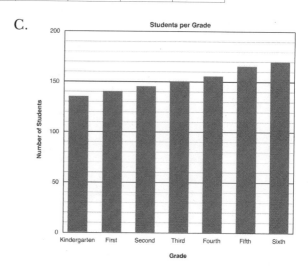

B.

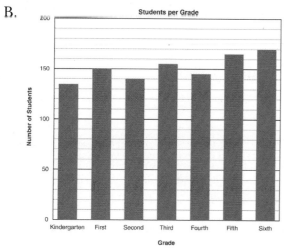

D.

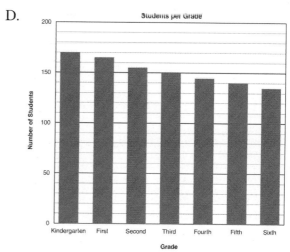

6. A gymnastics team has the following scores for an event: 12.3, 12.7, 14.1, 14.5, 13.8, 13.6, 14.2, 15.2, 14.8, 13.9, 15.4, 14.3. Find the mean score for the team to the nearest hundredth.

   A. 14.07 C. 14.57

   B. 14.15 D. 14.71

7. Perform the operation, $(8x^2-6x-3)-(4x^2-5x+4)$.

   A. $4x^2-11x-7$ C. $4x^2-x-7$

   B. $4x^2-11x+1$ D. $4x^2-x+1$

8. Apply the polynomial identity to rewrite $9x^2-30x+25$.

   A. $(3x+5)(3x-5)$ C. $(3x-5)(3x-1)$

   B. $(3x-5)^2$ D. $(3x-5)(3x+1)$

9. Simplify $(4x^3)^2$.

   A. $8x^5$ C. $16x^5$

   B. $8x^6$ D. $16x^6$

10. The landmass of the United States is about 4×10^6 square miles, and the landmass of Alaska is about 7×10^5 square miles. How many times larger is the landmass of the United States than the landmass of Alaska?

    A. 1 C. 4

    B. 3 D. 6

11. When would non-probability sampling be used to study the characteristics of a state population?

    A. Demonstrate existing traits

    B. Studies with the nth person selected

    C. Studies with a limited amount of time

    D. Divide population into groups and obtain a sample

12. A school wants to know the daily attendance of all classes. What data would be good for a census?

    A. Attendance on Fridays

    B. Attendance every day

    C. Attendance for math classes

    D. Attendance after holiday breaks

13. A toy bin contains 12 yellow balls, 3 orange balls, and 5 white balls. What is the probability of selecting an orange or a white ball?

    A. $\frac{3}{80}$ C. $\frac{1}{4}$

    B. $\frac{3}{20}$ D. $\frac{2}{5}$

14. A cell phone company projects $\frac{1}{2}$ of making $3 million, $\frac{3}{10}$ of making $1 million, and $\frac{1}{5}$ of losing $2 million. What is the expected value?

    A. $1.4 million

    B. $1.5 million

    C. $1.8 million

    D. $2.0 million

CHAPTER 2 ALGEBRA
PRACTICE QUIZ 2 – ANSWER KEY

1. C. The correct solution is 6.

$\frac{x}{2} = 3$	Subtract 5 from both sides of the equation.
$x = 6$	Multiply both sides of the equation by 2.

See Lesson: Equations with One Variable.

2. D. The correct solution is $\frac{9}{2}$.

$5x-3=3x+6$	Combine like terms on the left and right sides of the equation.
$2x-3=6$	Subtract $3x$ from both sides of the equation.
$2x=9$	Add 3 to both sides of the equation.
	Divide both sides of the equation by 2.

See Lesson: Equations with One Variable.

3. D. The correct solution is (-9, 5).

$-6x-2y=44$	Multiply all terms in the second equation by -2.
$-8x=72$	Add the equations.
$x=-9$	Divide both sides of the equation by -8.
$3(-9)+y=-22$	Substitute -9 in the second equation for x.
$-27+y=-22$	Simplify using order of operations.
$y=5$	Add 27 to both sides of the equation.

See Lesson: Equations with Two Variables.

4. C. The correct graph has the two lines intersect at (-9, -1). **See Lesson: Equations with Two Variables.**

5. B. The correct solution is B because the number of students for each grade is correct. **See Lesson: Interpreting Graphics.**

6. A. The correct solution is 14.07. The sum of the scores is 168.8, and the average is 14.07 for the 12 scores. **See Lesson: Interpreting Graphics.**

7. C. The correct solution is $4x^2-x-7$.

$$(8x^2-6x-3)-(4x^2-5x+4) = (8x^2-6x-3) + (-4x^2 + 5x-4) = (8x^2-4x^2) + (-6x + 5x) + (-3-4) = 4x^2-x-7$$

See Lesson: Polynomials.

8. B. The correct solution is $(3x-5)^2$. The expression $9x^2-30x+25$ is rewritten as $(3x-5)^2$ because the value of a is $3x$ and the value of b is 5. **See Lesson: Polynomials.**

9. D. The correct solution is $16x^6$ because $(4x^3)^2 = 4^2 x^{3\times2} = 4^2 x^6 = 16x^6$. **See Lesson: Powers, Exponents, Roots, and Radicals.**

10. D. The correct solution is 6 because the landmass of the United States is about 4,000,000 square miles and the landmass of Alaska is about 700,000 square miles. So, the United States is about 6 times larger. **See Lesson: Powers, Exponents, Roots, and Radicals.**

11. C. The correct solution is studies with a limited amount of time because this is a non-random process. **See Lesson: Statistical Measures.**

12. B. The correct solution is attendance every day because data is collected from every class every day. **See Lesson: Statistical Measures.**

13. D. The correct solution is $\frac{2}{5}$. There are 3 orange balls and 5 white balls out of 20 total balls. The probability is $\frac{3}{20} + \frac{5}{20} = \frac{8}{20} = \frac{2}{5}$. **See Lesson: Statistics & Probability: The Rules of Probability.**

14. A. The correct solution is \$1.4 million. The expected value is $\frac{1}{2}(3) + \frac{3}{10}(1) + \frac{1}{5}(-2) = 1.5 + 0.3 - 0.4 = \$1.4$ million. **See Lesson: Statistics & Probability: The Rules of Probability.**

CHAPTER 3 ADVANCED ALGEBRA AND GEOMETRY

FACTORS AND MULTIPLES

This lesson shows the relationship between factors and multiples of a number. In addition, it introduces prime and composite numbers and demonstrates how to use prime factorization to determine all the factors of a number.

Factors of a Number

Multiplication converts two or more factors into a product. A given number, however, may be the product of more than one combination of factors; for example, 12 is the product of 3 and 4 and the product of 2 and 6. Limiting consideration to the set of whole numbers, a **factor of a number** (call it x) is a whole number whose product with any other whole number is equal to x. For instance, 2 is a factor of 12 because $12 \div 2$ is a whole number (6). Another way of expressing it is that 2 is a factor of 12 because 12 is **divisible** by 2.

> **BE CAREFUL!**
> The term *factor* can mean any number being multiplied by another number, or it can mean a number by which another number is divisible. The two uses are related but slightly different. The context will generally clarify which meaning applies.

A whole number always has at least two factors: 1 and itself. That is, for any whole number y, $1 \times y = y$. To test whether one number is a factor of a second number, divide the second by the first. If the quotient is whole, it is a factor. If the quotient is not whole (or it has a remainder), it is not a factor.

Example

Which number is not a factor of 54?

A. 1   B. 2   C. 4   D. 6

The correct answer is **C**. A number is a factor of another number if the latter is divisible by the former. The number 54 is divisible by 1 because $54 \times 1 = 54$, and it is divisible by 2 because $27 \times 2 = 54$. Also, $6 \times 9 = 54$. But $54 \div 4 = 13.5$ (or 13R2). Therefore, 4 is not a factor.

Multiples of a Number

Multiples of a number are related to factors of a number. A **multiple of a number** is that number's product with some integer. For example, if a hardware store sells a type of screw that only comes in packs of 20, customers must buy these screws in *multiples* of 20: that is, 20, 40, 60, 80, and so on. (Technically, 0 is also a multiple.) These numbers are equal to 20×1, $20 \times$

2, 20 × 3, 20 × 4, and so on. Similarly, measurements in feet represent multiples of 12 inches. A (whole-number) measurement in feet would be equivalent to 12 inches, 24 inches, 36 inches, and so on.

When counting by twos or threes, multiples are used. But because the multiples of a number are the product of that number with the integers, multiples can also be negative. For the number 2, the multiples are the set {..., −6, −4, −2, 0, 2, 4, 6,...}, where the ellipsis dots indicate that the set continues the pattern indefinitely in both directions. Also, the number can be any real number: the multiples of π (approximately 3.14) are {..., −3π, −2π, −1π, 0, 1π, 2π, 3π,...}. Note that the notation 2π, for example, means 2 × π.

The positive multiples (along with 0) of a whole number are all numbers for which that whole number is a factor. For instance, the positive multiples of 5 are 0, 5, 10, 15, 20, 25, 30, and so on. That full set contains all (whole) numbers for which 5 is a factor. Thus, one number is a multiple of a second number if the second number is a factor of the first.

Example

If a landowner subdivides a parcel of property into multiples of 7 acres, how many acres can a buyer purchase?

A. 1   B. 15   C. 29   D. 42

The correct answer is **D**. Because the landowner subdivides the property into multiples of 7 acres, a buyer must choose an acreage from the list 7 acres, 14 acres, 21 acres, and so on. That list includes 42 acres. Another way to solve the problem is to find which answer is divisible by 7 (that is, which number has 7 as a factor).

Prime and Composite Numbers

For some real-world applications, such as cryptography, factors and multiples play an important role. One important way to classify whole numbers is by whether they are prime or composite. A **prime** number is any whole (or natural) number greater than 1 that has only itself and 1 as factors. The smallest example is 2: because 2 only has 1 and 2 as factors, it is prime. **Composite** numbers have at least one factor other than 1 and themselves. The smallest composite number is 4: in addition to 1 and 4, it has 2 as a factor.

Determining whether a number is prime can be extremely difficult—hence its value in cryptography. One simple test that works for some numbers is to check whether the number is even or odd. An **even number** is divisible by 2; an **odd number** is not. To determine whether a number is even or odd, look at the last (rightmost) digit.

BE CAREFUL!
Avoid the temptation to call 1 a prime number. Although it only has itself and 1 as factors, those factors are the same number. Hence, 1 is fundamentally different from the prime numbers, which start at 2.

If that digit is even (0, 2, 4, 6, or 8), the number is even. Otherwise, it is odd. Another simple test works for multiples of 3. Add all the digits in the number. If the sum is divisible by 3, the original number is also divisible by 3. This rule can be successively applied multiple times until the sum of digits is manageable. That number is then composite.

Example

Which number is prime?

A. 6   B. 16   C. 61   D. 116

The correct answer is **C**. When applicable, the easiest way to identify a number greater than 2 as composite rather than prime is to check whether it is even. All even numbers greater than 2 are composite. By elimination, 61 is prime.

Prime Factorization

Determining whether a number is prime, even for relatively small numbers (less than 100), can be difficult. One tool that can help both solve this problem and identify all factors of a number is **prime factorization**. One way to do prime factorization is to make a **factor tree**.

The procedure below demonstrates the process.

STEP BY STEP

Step 1. Write the number you want to factor.

Step 2. If the number is prime, stop. Otherwise, go to Step 3.

Step 3. Find any two factors of the number and write them on the line below the number.

Step 4. "Connect" the factors and the number using line segments. The result will look somewhat like an inverted tree, particularly as the process continues.

Step 5. Repeat Steps 2–4 for all composite factors in the tree.

The numbers in the factor tree are either "branches" (if they are connected downward to other numbers) or "leaves" (if they have no further downward connections). The leaves constitute all the prime factors of the original number: when multiplied together, their product is that number. Moreover, any product of two or more of the leaves is a factor of the original number. Thus, using prime factorization helps find any and all factors of a number, although the process can be tedious when performed by hand (particularly for large numbers). Below is a factor tree for the number 96. All the leaves are circled for emphasis.

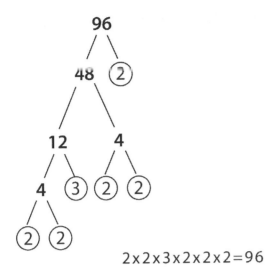

$$2 \times 2 \times 3 \times 2 \times 2 \times 2 = 96$$

Example

Which list includes all the unique prime factors of 84?

A. 2, 3, 7   B. 3, 4, 7   C. 3, 5, 7   D. 1, 2, 3, 7

The correct answer is **A**. One approach is to find the prime factorization of 84. The factor tree shows that $84 = 2 \times 2 \times 3 \times 7$. Alternatively, note that answer D includes 1, which is not prime. Answer B includes 4, which is a composite number. Since answer C includes 5, which is not a factor of 84, the only possible answer is A.

Let's Review!

- A whole number is divisible by all of its factors, which are also whole numbers by definition.
- Multiples of a number are all possible products of that number and the integers.
- A prime number is a whole number greater than 1 that has no factors other than itself and 1.
- A composite number is a whole number greater than 1 that is not prime (that is, it has factors other than itself and 1).
- Even numbers are divisible by 2; odd numbers are not.
- Prime factorization yields all the prime factors of a number. The factor-tree method is one way to determine prime factorization.

SOLVING QUADRATIC EQUATIONS

This lesson introduces solving quadratic equations by the square root method, completing the square, factoring, and using the quadratic formula.

Solving Quadratic Equations by the Square Root Method

A **quadratic equation** is an equation where the highest variable is squared. The equation is in the form $ax^2 + bx + c = 0$, where a is a non-zero constant and b and c are constants. There are at most two solutions to the equation because the highest variable is squared. There are many methods to solve a quadratic equation.

This section will explore solving a quadratic equation by the square root method. The equation must be in the form of $ax^2 = c$, or there is no x term.

STEP BY STEP

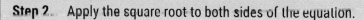

Step 1. Use multiplication and division properties of an equation to remove the value in front of the variable.

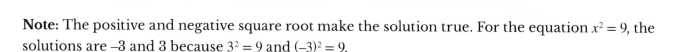

Step 2. Apply the square root to both sides of the equation.

Note: The positive and negative square root make the solution true. For the equation $x^2 = 9$, the solutions are –3 and 3 because $3^2 = 9$ and $(-3)^2 = 9$.

Example

Solve the equation by the square root method, $4x^2 = 64$.

A. 4   B. 8   C. ±4   D. ±8

The correct answer is **C**. The correct solution is ±4.

$x^2 = 16$ Divide both sides of the equation by 4.

$x = \pm 4$ Apply the square root to both sides of the equation.

Solving Quadratic Equations by Completing the Square

A quadratic equation in the form $x^2 + bx$ can be solved by a process known as completing the square. The best time to solve by completing the square is when the b term is even.

> **STEP BY STEP**
>
> **Step 1.** Divide all terms by the coefficient of x^2.
>
> **Step 2.** Move the number term to the right side of the equation.
>
> **Step 3.** Complete the square $\left(\frac{b}{2}\right)^2$ and add this value to both sides of the equation.
>
> **Step 4.** Factor the left side of the equation.
>
> **Step 5.** Apply the square root to both sides of the equation.
>
> **Step 6.** Use addition and subtraction properties to move all number terms to the right side of the equation.

Examples

1. **Solve the equation by completing the square, $x^2 - 8x + 12 = 0$.**

    A. -2 and -6 B. 2 and -6 C. -2 and 6 D. 2 and 6

    The correct answer is **D**. The correct solutions are 2 and 6.

$x^2 - 8x = -12$	Subtract 12 from both sides of the equation.
$x^2 - 8x + 16 = -12 + 16$	Complete the square, $\left(-\frac{8}{2}\right)^2 = (-4)^2 = 16$.
	Add 16 to both sides of the equation.
$x^2 - 8x + 16 = 4$	Simplify the right side of the equation.
$(x-4)^2 = 4$	Factor the left side of the equation.
$x - 4 = \pm 2$	Apply the square root to both sides of the equation.
$x = 4 \pm 2$	Add 4 to both sides of the equation.
$x = 4 - 2 = 2,\ x = 4 + 2 = 6$	Simplify the right side of the equation.

2. **Solve the equation by completing the square, $x^2 + 6x - 8 = 0$.**

    A. $-3 \pm \sqrt{17}$ B. $3 \pm \sqrt{17}$ C. $-3 \pm \sqrt{8}$ D. $3 \pm \sqrt{8}$

    The correct answer is **A**. The correct solutions are $-3 \pm \sqrt{17}$.

$x^2 + 6x = 8$	Add 8 to both sides of the equation.
$x^2 + 6x + 9 = 8 + 9$	Complete the square, $\left(\frac{6}{2}\right)^2 = 3^2 = 9$. Add 9 to both sides of the equation.
$x^2 + 6x + 9 = 17$	Simplify the right side of the equation.
$(x + 3)^2 = 17$	Factor the left side of the equation.
$x + 3 = \pm\sqrt{17}$	Apply the square root to both sides of the equation.
$x = -3 \pm \sqrt{17}$	Subtract 3 from both sides of the equation.

Solving Quadratic Equations by Factoring

Factoring can only be used when a quadratic equation is factorable; other methods are needed to solve quadratic equations that are not factorable.

> **STEP BY STEP**
>
> **Step 1.** Simplify if needed by clearing any fractions and parentheses.
>
> **Step 2.** Write the equation in standard form, $ax^2 + bx + c = 0$.
>
> **Step 3.** Factor the quadratic equation.
>
> **Step 4.** Set each factor equal to zero.
>
> **Step 5.** Solve the linear equations using inverse operations.

The quadratic equation will have two solutions if the factors are different or one solution if the factors are the same.

Examples

1. **Solve the equation by factoring, $x^2 - 13x + 42 = 0$.**

   A. $-6, -7$ B. $-6, 7$ C. $6, -7$ D. $6, 7$

   The correct answer is **D**. The correct solutions are 6 and 7.

$(x-6)(x-7) = 0$	Factor the equation.
$(x-6) = 0$ or $(x-7) = 0$	Set each factor equal to 0.
$x-6 = 0$	Add 6 to both sides of the equation to solve for the first factor.
$x = 6$	
$x-7 = 0$	Add 7 to both sides of the equation to solve for the second factor.
$x = 7$	

2. **Solve the equation by factoring, $9x^2 + 30x + 25 = 0$.**

   A. $-\frac{5}{3}$ B. $-\frac{3}{5}$ C. $\frac{3}{5}$ D. $\frac{5}{3}$

   The correct answer is **A**. The correct solution is $-\frac{5}{3}$.

$(3x + 5)(3x + 5) = 0$	Factor the equation.
$(3x + 5) = 0$ or $(3x + 5) = 0$	Set each factor equal to 0.
$(3x + 5) = 0$	Set one factor equal to zero since both factors are the same.
$3x + 5 = 0$	Subtract 5 from both sides of the equation and divide both sides of the equation by 3 to solve.
$3x = -5$	
$x = -\frac{5}{3}$	

Solving Quadratic Equations by the Quadratic Formula

Many quadratic equations are not factorable. Another method of solving a quadratic equation is by using the quadratic formula. This method can be used to solve any quadratic equation in the form . Using the coefficients a, b, and c, the quadratic formula is $x = \frac{-b \pm \sqrt{b^2 - 4ac}}{2a}$. The values are substituted into the formula, and applying the order of operations finds the solution(s) to the equation.

The solution of the quadratic formula in these examples will be exact or estimated to three decimal places. There may be cases where the exact solutions to the quadratic formula are used.

KEEP IN MIND

Watch the negative sign in the formula. Remember that a number squared is always positive.

Examples

1. **Solve the equation by the quadratic formula, $x^2 - 5x - 6 = 0$.**

    A. –6 and –1   B. 6 and –1   C. –6 and 1   D. 6 and 1

    The correct answer is **B**. The correct solutions are 6 and –1.

    $x = \frac{-(-5) \pm \sqrt{(-5)^2 - 4(1)(-6)}}{2(1)}$ Substitute 1 for a, –5 for b, and –6 for c.

    $x = \frac{5 \pm \sqrt{25 - (-24)}}{2}$ Apply the exponent and perform the multiplication.

    $x = \frac{5 \pm \sqrt{49}}{2}$ Perform the subtraction.

    $x = \frac{5 \pm 7}{2}$ Apply the square root.

    $x = \frac{5 + 7}{2}, \ x = \frac{5 - 7}{2}$ Separate the problem into two expressions.

    $x = \frac{12}{2} = 6, \ x = \frac{-2}{2} = -1$ Simplify the numerator and divide.

2. **Solve the equation by the quadratic formula, $2x^2 + 4x - 5 = 0$.**

    A. –5.74 and –1.74   B. 5.74 and –1.74   C. –5.74 and 1.74   D. 5.74 and 1.74

    The correct answer is **C**. The correct solutions are –5.74 and 1.74.

    $x = \frac{-4 \pm \sqrt{4^2 - 4(2)(-5)}}{2(2)}$ Substitute 2 for a, 4 for b, and –5 for c.

    $x = \frac{-4 \pm \sqrt{16 - (-40)}}{4}$ Apply the exponent and perform the multiplication.

    $x = \frac{-4 \pm \sqrt{56}}{4}$ Perform the subtraction.

    $x = \frac{-4 \pm 7.48}{2}$ Apply the square root.

    $x = \frac{-4 + 7.48}{2}, \ x = \frac{-4 - 7.48}{2}$ Separate the problem into two expressions.

    $x = \frac{3.48}{2} = 1.74, \ x = \frac{-11.48}{2} = -5.74$ Simplify the numerator and divide.

Let's Review!

There are four methods to solve a quadratic equation algebraically:

- The square root method is used when there is a squared variable term and a constant term.
- Completing the square is used when there is a squared variable term and an even variable term.
- Factoring is used when the equation can be factored.
- The quadratic formula can be used for any quadratic equation.

CONGRUENCE

This lesson discusses basic terms for geometry. Many polygons have the property of lines of symmetry, or rotational symmetry. Rotations, reflections, and translations are ways to create congruent polygons.

Geometry Terms

The terms *point*, *line*, and *plane* help define other terms in geometry. A point is an exact location in space with no size and has a label with a capital letter. A line has location and direction, is always straight, and has infinitely many points that extend in both directions. A plane has infinitely many intersecting lines that extend forever in all directions.

The diagram shows point W, point X, point Y, and point Z. The line is labeled as $\overleftrightarrow{WX}$, and the plane is Plane A or Plane WYZ (or any three points in the plane).

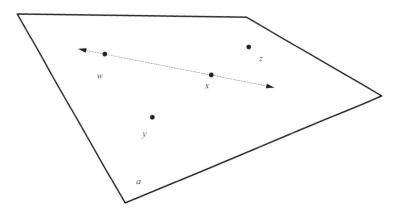

With these definitions, many other geometry terms can be defined. *Collinear* is a term for points that lie on the same line, and *coplanar* is a term for points and/or lines within the same plane. A line segment is a part of a line with two endpoints. For example, $\overline{WX}$ has endpoints W and X. A ray has an endpoint and extends forever in one direction. For example, $\longrightarrow AB$ has an endpoint of A, and $\longrightarrow BA$ has an endpoint of B. The intersection of lines, planes, segment, or rays is a point or a set of points.

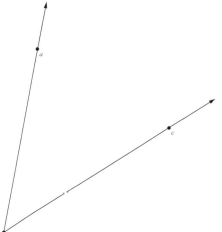

Some key statements that are evident in geometry are

- There is exactly one straight line through any two points.
- There is exactly one plane that contains any three non-collinear points.
- A line with points in the plane lies in the plane.
- Two lines intersect at a point.
- Two planes intersect at a line.

Two rays that share an endpoint form an angle. The vertex is the common endpoint of the two rays that form an angle. When naming an angle, the vertex is the center point. The angle below is named ∠ABC or ∠CBA.

An acute angle has a measure between 0° and 90°, and a 90° angle is a right angle. An obtuse angle has a measure between 90° and 180°, and a 180° angle is a straight angle.

There are two special sets of lines. Parallel lines are at least two lines that never intersect within the same plane. Perpendicular lines intersect at one point and form four angles.

Example

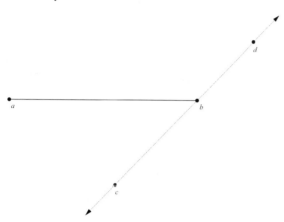

BE CAREFUL!
Lines are always named with two points, a plane can be named with three points, and an angle is named with the vertex as the center point.

Describe the diagram.

A. Points A, B, C, and D are collinear.

B. Points A, C, and D are collinear.

C. $\overline{CD}$ intersects $\overleftrightarrow{AB}$ at point B.

D. $\overline{AB}$ intersects $\overleftrightarrow{CD}$ at point B.

The correct answer is **D**. The correct solution is $\overline{AB}$ intersects $\overleftrightarrow{CD}$ at point B. The segment intersects the line at point B.

Line and Rotational Symmetry

Symmetry is a reflection or rotation of a shape that allows that shape to be carried onto itself. Line symmetry, or reflection symmetry, is when two halves of a shape are reflected onto each other across a line. A shape may have none, one, or several lines of symmetry. A kite has one line of symmetry, and a scalene triangle has no lines of symmetry.

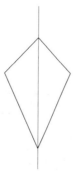
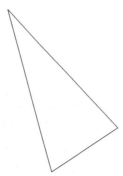

Rotational symmetry is when a figure can be mapped onto itself by a rotation about a point through any angle between 0° and 360°. The order of rotational symmetry is the number of times the object can be rotated. If there is no rotational symmetry, the order is 1 because the object can only be rotated 360° to map the figure onto itself. A square has 90° rotational symmetry and is order 4 because it can be rotated 90°, 180°, 270°, and 360°. A trapezoid has no rotational symmetry and is order 1 because it can only be rotated 360° to map onto itself.

KEEP IN MIND

A polygon can have both, neither, or either reflection and rotational symmetry.

Example

What is the rotational symmetry for a regular octagon?

A. 30°   B. 45°   C. 60°   D. 75°

The correct answer is **B**. The correct solution is 45°. For a regular polygon, divide 360° by the eight sides of the octagon to obtain 45°.

Rotations, Reflections, and Translations

There are three types of transformations: rotations, reflections, and translations. A rotation is a turn of a figure about a point in a given direction. A reflection is a flip over a line of symmetry, and a translation is a slide horizontally, vertically, or both. Each of these transformations produces a congruent image.

A rotation changes ordered pairs (x, y) in the coordinate plane. A 90° rotation counterclockwise about the point becomes $(-y, x)$, a 180° rotation counterclockwise about the point becomes $(-x, -y)$, and a 270° rotation the point becomes $(y, -x)$. Using the point $(6, -8)$,

- 90° rotation counterclockwise about the origin $(8, 6)$
- 180° rotation counterclockwise about the origin $(-6, 8)$
- 270° rotation counterclockwise about the origin $(-8, -6)$

A reflection also changes ordered pairs (x, y) in the coordinate plane. A reflection across the x-axis changes the sign of the y-coordinate, and a reflection across the y-axis changes the sign of the x-coordinate. A reflection over the line $y = x$ changes the points to (y, x), and a reflection over the line $y = -x$ changes the points to $(-y, -x)$. Using the point $(6, -8)$,

- A reflection across the x-axis $(6, 8)$
- A reflection across the y-axis $(-6, -8)$
- A reflection over the line $y = x$ $(-8, 6)$
- A reflection over the line $y = -x$ $(8, -6)$

A translation changes ordered pairs (x, y) left or right and/or up or down. Adding a positive value to an x-coordinate is a translation to the right, and adding a negative value to an x-coordinate is a translation to the left. Adding a positive value to

KEEP IN MIND

A rotation is a turn, a reflection is a flip, and a translation is a slide.

a y-coordinate is a translation up, and adding a negative value to a y-coordinate is a translation down. Using the point $(6, -8)$,

- A translation of $(x + 3)$ is a translation right 3 units $(9, -8)$
- A translation of $(x - 3)$ is a translation left 3 units $(3, -8)$
- A translation of $(y + 3)$ is a translation up 3 units $(6, -5)$
- A translation of $(y - 3)$ is a translation down 3 units $(6, -11)$

Example

$\triangle ABC$ has points A $(3, -2)$, B $(2, -1)$, and C $(-1, 4)$, which after a transformation become A' $(2, 3)$, B' $(1, 2)$, and C' $(-4, -1)$. What is the transformation between the points?

A. Reflection across the x-axis

B. Reflection across the y-axis

C. Rotation of 90° counterclockwise

D. Rotation of 270° counterclockwise

The correct answer is **C**. The correct solution is a rotation of 90° counterclockwise because the points (x, y) become $(y, -x)$.

Let's Review!

- The terms *point*, *line*, and *plane* help define many terms in geometry.
- Symmetry allows a figure to carry its shape onto itself. This can be reflectional or rotational symmetry.
- Three transformations are rotation (turn), reflection (flip), and translation (slide).

SIMILARITY, RIGHT TRIANGLES, AND TRIGONOMETRY

This lesson defines and applies terminology associated with coordinate planes. It also demonstrates how to find the area of two-dimensional shapes and the surface area and volume of three-dimensional cubes and right prisms.

Coordinate Plane

The **coordinate plane** is a two-dimensional number line with the horizontal axis called the **x-axis** and the vertical axis called the **y-axis**. Each **ordered pair** or **coordinate** is listed as (x, y). The center point is the origin and has an ordered pair of $(0, 0)$. A coordinate plane has four quadrants.

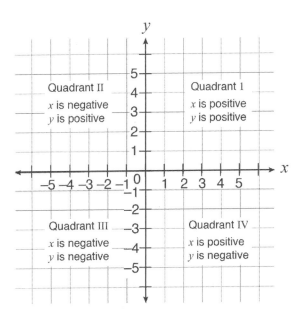

KEEP IN MIND

The x-coordinates are positive to the right of the y-axis. The y-coordinates are positive above the x-axis.

To graph a point in the coordinate plane, start with the x-coordinate. This point states the number of steps to the left (negative) or to the right (positive) from the origin. Then, the y-coordinate states the number of steps up (positive) or down (negative) from the x-coordinate.

Given a set of ordered pairs, points can be drawn in the coordinate plane to create polygons. The length of a segment can be found if the segment has the same first coordinate or the same second coordinate.

Examples

1. **Draw a triangle with the coordinates (–2, –1), (–3, 5), (–4, 2).**

A.

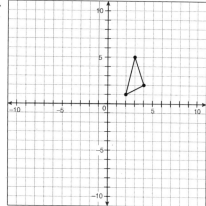

C.

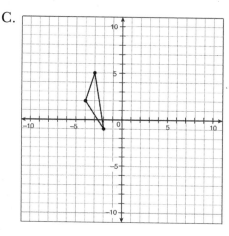

B.

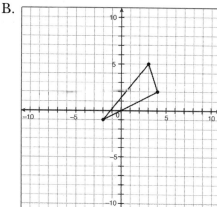

D.

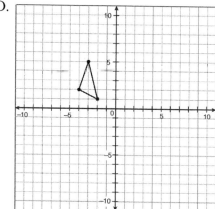

The correct answer is **C**. The first point is in the third quadrant because x is negative and y is negative, and the last two points are in the second quadrant because x is negative and y is positive.

2. **Given the coordinates for a rectangle (4, 8), (4, –2), (–1, –2) (–1, 8), find the length of each side of the rectangle.**

   A. 3 units and 6 units

   B. 3 units and 10 units

   C. 5 units and 6 units

   D. 5 units and 10 units

   The correct answer is **D**. The correct solution is 5 units and 10 units. The difference between the x-coordinates is $4-(-1) = 5$ units, and the difference between the y-coordinates is $8-(-2) = 10$ units.

3. **The dimensions for a soccer field are 45 meters by 90 meters. One corner of a soccer field on the coordinate plane is (–45, –30). What could a second coordinate be?**

   A. (–45, 30)   B. (–45, 45)   C. (–45, 60)   D. (–45, 75)

   The correct answer is **C**. The correct solution is (–45, 60) because 90 can be added to the y-coordinate, $-30 + 90 = 60$.

Area of Two-Dimensional Objects

The **area** is the number of unit squares that fit inside a two-dimensional object. A unit square is one unit long by one unit wide, which includes 1 foot by 1 foot and 1 meter by 1 meter. The unit of measurement for area is units squared (or feet squared, meters squared, and so on). The following are formulas for calculating the area of various shapes.

BE CAREFUL!

Make sure that you apply the correct formula for area of each two-dimensional object.

- Rectangle: The product of the length and the width, $A = lw$.
- Parallelogram: The product of the base and the height, $A = bh$.
- Square: The side length squared, $A = s^2$.
- Triangle: The product of one-half the base and the height, $A = \frac{1}{2}bh$.
- Trapezoid: The product of one-half the height and the sum of the bases, $A = \frac{1}{2}h(b_1 + b_2)$.
- Regular polygon: The product of one-half the **apothem** (a line from the center of the regular polygon that is perpendicular to a side) and the sum of the perimeter, $A = \frac{1}{2}ap$.

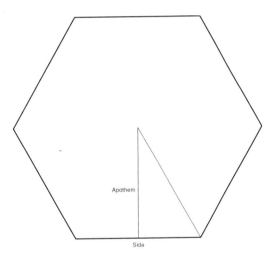

Apothem

Side

Examples

1. **A trapezoid has a height of 3 centimeters and bases of 8 centimeters and 10 centimeters. Find the area in square centimeters.**

    A. 18   B. 27   C. 52   D. 55

    The correct answer is **B**. The correct solution is 27. Substitute the values into the formula and simplify using the order of operations, $A = \frac{1}{2}h(b_1 + b_2) = \frac{1}{2}(3)(8 + 10) = \frac{1}{2}(3)(18) = 27$ square centimeters.

2. **A regular decagon has a side length of 12 inches and an apothem of 6 inches. Find the area in square inches.**

    A. 120   B. 360   C. 720   D. 960

    The correct answer is **B**. The correct solution is 360. Simplify using the order of operations, $A = \frac{1}{2}ap = \frac{1}{2}(6)(12(10)) = 360$ square inches.

3. Two rectangular rooms need to be carpeted. The dimensions of the first room are 18 feet by 19 feet, and the dimensions of the second room are 12 feet by 10 feet. What is the total area to be carpeted in square feet?

   A. 118   B. 236   C. 342   D. 462

   The correct answer is **D**. The correct solution is 462. Substitute the values into the formula and simplify using the order of operations, $A = lw + lw = 18(19) + 12(10) = 342 + 120 = 462$ square feet.

4. A picture frame is in the shape of a right triangle with legs 12 centimeters and 13 centimeters and hypotenuse of 17 centimeters. What is the area in square centimeters?

   A. 78   B. 108   C. 117   D. 156

   The correct answer is **A**. The correct solution is 78. Substitute the values into the formula and simplify using the order of operations, $A = \frac{1}{2}bh = \frac{1}{2}(12)(13) = 78$ square centimeters.

Surface Area and Volume of Cubes and Right Prisms

A three-dimensional object has length, width, and height. **Cubes** are made up of six congruent square faces. A **right prism** is made of three sets of congruent faces, with at least two sets of congruent rectangles.

> **BE CAREFUL!**
> Surface area is a two-dimensional calculation, and volume is a three-dimensional calculation.

The **surface area** of any three-dimensional object is the sum of the area of all faces. The formula for the surface area of a cube is $SA = 6s^2$ because there are six congruent faces. For a right rectangular prism, the surface area formula is $SA = 2lw + 2lh + 2hw$ because there are three sets of congruent rectangles. For a triangular prism, the surface area formula is twice the area of the base plus the area of the other three rectangles that make up the prism.

The **volume** of any three-dimensional object is the amount of space inside the object. The volume formula for a cube is $V = s^3$. The volume formula for a rectangular prism is the area of the base times the height, or $V = Bh$.

Examples

1. A cube has a side length of 5 centimeters. What is the surface area in square centimeters?

   A. 20   B. 25   C. 125   D. 150

   The correct answer is **D**. The correct solution is 150. Substitute the values into the formula and simplify using the order of operations, $SA = 6s^2 = 6(5^2) = 6(25) = 150$ square centimeters.

2. A cube has a side length of 5 centimeters. What is the volume in cubic centimeters?

   A. 20   B. 25   C. 125   D. 180

   The correct answer is **C**. The correct solution is 125. Substitute the values into the formula and simplify using the order of operations, $V = s^3 = 5^3 = 125$ cubic centimeters.

3. A right rectangular prism has dimensions of 4 inches by 5 inches by 6 inches. What is the surface area in square inches?

    A. 60   B. 74   C. 120   D. 148

    The correct answer is **D**. The correct solution is 148. Substitute the values into the formula and simplify using the order of operations, $SA = 2lw + 2lh + 2hw = 2(4)(5) + 2(4)(6) + 2(6)(5) = 40 + 48 + 60 = 148$ square inches.

4. A right rectangular prism has dimensions of 4 inches by 5 inches by 6 inches. What is the volume in cubic inches?

    A. 60   B. 62   C. 120   D. 124

    The correct answer is **C**. The correct solution is 120. Substitute the values into the formula and simplify using the order of operations, $V = lwh = 4(5)(6) = 120$ cubic inches.

Let's Review!

- The coordinate plane is a two-dimensional number line that is used to display ordered pairs. Two-dimensional shapes can be drawn on the plane, and the length of the objects can be determined based on the given coordinates.
- The area of a two-dimensional object is the amount of space inside the shape. There are area formulas to use to calculate the area of various shapes.
- For a three-dimensional object, the surface area is the sum of the area of the faces and the volume is the amount of space inside the object. Cubes and right rectangular prisms are common three-dimensional solids.

CIRCLES

This lesson introduces concepts of circles, including finding the circumference and the area of the circle.

Circle Terminology

A **circle** is a figure composed of points that are equidistant from a given point. The **center** is the point from which all points are equidistant. A **chord** is a segment whose endpoints are on the circle, and the **diameter** is a chord that goes through the center of the circle. The **radius** is a segment with one endpoint at the center of the circle and one endpoint on the circle. **Arcs** have two endpoints on the circle and all points on a circle between those endpoints.

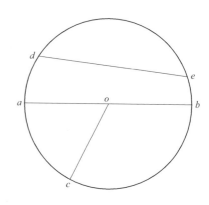

In the circle at the right, O is the center, $\overline{OC}$ is the radius, $\overline{AB}$ is the diameter, $\overline{DE}$ is a chord, and $\overparen{AD}$ is an arc.

Example

Identify a diameter of the circle.

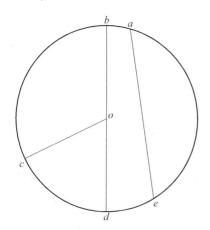

KEEP IN MIND

The radius is one-half the length of the diameter of the circle.

A. $\overline{BD}$ B. $\overline{OC}$ C. $\overline{DO}$ D. $\overline{AE}$

The correct answer is **A**. The correct solution is $\overline{BD}$ because points B and D are on the circle and the segment goes through the center O.

Circumference and Area of a Circle

The **circumference** of a circle is the perimeter, or the distance, around the circle. There are two ways to find the circumference. The formulas are the product of the diameter and pi or the product of twice the radius and pi. In symbol form, the formulas are $C = \pi d$ or $C = 2\pi r$.

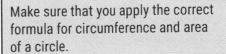

BE CAREFUL!

Make sure that you apply the correct formula for circumference and area of a circle.

The **area** of a circle is the amount of space inside a circle. The formula is the product of pi and the radius squared. In symbol form, the formula is $A = \pi r^2$. The area is always expressed in square units.

Given the circumference or the area of a circle, the radius and the diameter can be determined. The given measurement is substituted into the appropriate formula. Then, the equation is solved for the radius or the diameter.

Examples

1. **Find the circumference in centimeters of a circle with a diameter of 8 centimeters. Use 3.14 for π.**

   A. 12.56   B. 25.12   C. 50.24   D. 100.48

   The correct answer is **B**. The correct solution is 25.12 because $C = \pi d \approx 3.14(8) \approx 25.12$ centimeters.

2. **Find the area in square inches of a circle with a radius of 15 inches. Use 3.14 for π.**

   A. 94.2   B. 176.63   C. 706.5   D. 828.96

   The correct answer is **C**. The correct solution is 706.5 because $A = \pi r^2 \approx 3.14(15)^2 \approx$

   $3.14(225) \approx 706.5$ square inches.

3. **A circle has a circumference of 70 centimeters. Find the diameter to the nearest tenth of a centimeter. Use 3.14 for π.**

   A. 11.1   B. 22.3   C. 33.5   D. 44.7

   The correct answer is **B**. The correct solution is 22.3 because $C = \pi d; 70 = 3.14d; d \approx 22.3$ centimeters.

4. **A circle has an area of 95 square centimeters. Find the radius to the nearest tenth of a centimeter. Use 3.14 for π.**

   A. 2.7   B. 5.5   C. 8.2   D. 10.9

   The correct answer is **B**. The correct solution is 5.5 because $A = \pi r^2; 95 = 3.14 r^2; 30.25 = r^2; r \approx 5.5$ centimeters.

Finding Circumference or Area Given the Other Value

Given the circumference of a circle, the area of the circle can be found. First, substitute the circumference into the formula and find the radius. Substitute the radius into the area formula and simplify.

Reverse the process to find the circumference given the area. First, substitute the area into the area formula and find the radius. Substitute the radius into the circumference formula and simplify.

BE CAREFUL!

Pay attention to the details with each formula and apply them in the correct order.

Examples

1. **The circumference of a circle is 45 inches. Find the area of the circle in square inches. Round to the nearest tenth. Use 3.14 for π.**

   A. 51.8   B. 65.1   C. 162.8   D. 204.5

   The correct answer is **C**. The correct solution is 162.8.

   $C = 2\pi r; 45 = 2(3.14)r; 45 = 6.28r; r \approx 7.2$ inches. $A = \pi r^2 \approx 3.14(7.2)^2 \approx 3.14(51.84) \approx 162.8$ square inches.

2. **The area of a circle is 60 square centimeters. Find the circumference of the circle in centimeters. Round to the nearest tenth. Use 3.14 for π.**

   A. 4.4   B. 13.8   C. 19.1   D. 27.6

   The correct answer is **D**. The correct solution is 27.6.

   $A = \pi r^2; 60 = 3.14 r^2; 19.11 = r^2; r \approx 4.4$ centimeters. $C = 2\pi r; C = 2(3.14)4.4 \approx 27.6$ centimeters.

Let's Review!

- Key terms related to circles are *radius, diameter, chord,* and *arc.* Note that the diameter is twice the radius.
- The circumference or the perimeter of a circle is the product of pi and the diameter or twice the radius and pi.
- The area of the circle is the product of pi and the radius squared.

MEASUREMENT AND DIMENSION

This lesson applies the formulas of volume for cylinders, pyramids, cones, and spheres to solve problems.

Volume of a Cylinder

A **cylinder** is a three-dimensional figure with two identical circular bases and a rectangular lateral face.

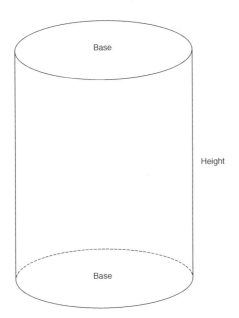

> **KEEP IN MIND**
> The volume of a cylinder can be expressed in terms of π, and the volume is measured in cubic units.

The volume of a cylinder equals the product of the area of the base and the height of the cylinder. This is the same formula used to calculate the volume of a right prism. In this case, the area of a base is a circle, so the formula is $V = Bh = \pi r^2 h$. The height is the perpendicular distance between the two circular bases.

Example

Find the volume of a cylinder in cubic centimeters with a radius of 13 centimeters and a height of 12 centimeters.

   A. 156π B. 312π C. $1{,}872\pi$ D. $2{,}028\pi$

The correct answer is **D**. The correct solution is $2{,}028\pi$. Substitute the values into the formula and simplify using the order of operations, $V = \pi r^2 h = \pi 13^2(12) = \pi(169)(12) = 2{,}028\pi$ cubic centimeters.

Volume of a Pyramid and a Cone

A **pyramid** is a three-dimensional solid with one base and all edges from the base meeting at the top, or apex. Pyramids can have any two-dimensional shape as the base. A **cone** is similar to a pyramid, but it has a circle instead of a polygon for the base.

BE CAREFUL!

Make sure that you apply the correct formula for area of the base for a pyramid.

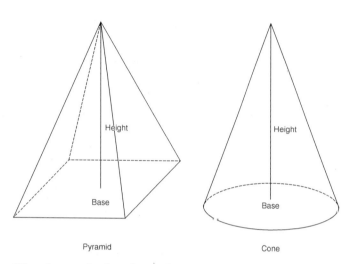

Pyramid   Cone

The formula for the volume of a pyramid is similar to a prism, $V = \frac{1}{3}Bh$ where B is the area of the base. The base is a circle for a cone, and the formula for the volume is $V = \frac{1}{3}Bh = \frac{1}{3}\pi r^2 h$.

Examples

1. **A regular hexagonal pyramid has base with side lengths of 5 centimeters and an apothem of 3 centimeters. If the height is 6 centimeters, find the volume in cubic centimeters.**

   A. 90   B. 180   C. 270   D. 360

   The correct answer is **A**. The correct solution is 90. Substitute the values into the formula and simplify using the order of operations, $V = \frac{1}{3}Bh = \frac{1}{3}(\frac{1}{2}ap)h = \frac{1}{3}(\frac{1}{2}(3)(30))6 = 90$ cubic centimeters.

2. **A cone has a radius of 10 centimeters and a height of 9 centimeters. Find the volume in cubic centimeters.**

   A. 270π B. 300π C. 810π D. 900π

   The correct answer is **B**. The correct solution is 300π. Substitute the values into the formula and simplify using the order of operations, $V = \frac{1}{3}\pi r^2 h = \frac{1}{3}\pi \, 10^2(9) = \frac{1}{3}\pi(100)(9) = 300\pi$ cubic centimeters.

Volume of a Sphere

A **sphere** is a round, three-dimensional solid, with every point on its surface equidistant to the center. The formula for the volume of a sphere is represented by just the radius of the sphere. The volume of a sphere is $V = \frac{4}{3}\pi r^3$. The volume of a hemi (half) of a sphere is $V = \left(\frac{1}{2}\right)\frac{4}{3}\pi r^3 = \frac{2}{3}\pi r^3$.

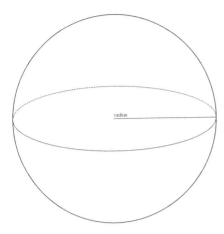

BE CAREFUL!

The radius is cubed, not squared, for the volume of a sphere.

Example

A sphere has a radius of 3 centimeters. Find the volume of a sphere in cubic centimeters.

A. 18π B. 27π C. 36π D. 45π

The correct answer is **C**. The correct solution is 36π. Substitute the values into the formula and simplify using the order of operations, $V = \frac{4}{3}\pi r^3 = \frac{4}{3}\pi 3^3 = \frac{4}{3}\pi(27) = 36\pi$ cubic centimeters.

Let's Review!

- The volume is the capacity of a three-dimensional object and is expressed in cubic units.
- The volume formula for a cylinder is the product of the area of the base (which is a circle) and the height of the cylinder.
- The volume formula for a pyramid or cone is one-third of the product of the area of the base (a circle in the case of the cone) and the height of the pyramid or cone.
- The volume formula for a sphere is $V = \frac{4}{3}\pi r^3$.

CHAPTER 3 ADVANCED ALGEBRA AND GEOMETRY
PRACTICE QUIZ 1

1. Half of a circular garden with a radius of 11.5 feet needs weeding. Find the area in square feet that needs weeding. Round to the nearest hundredth. Use 3.14 for π.

    A. 207.64   C. 519.08

    B. 415.27   D. 726.73

2. The area of a circle is 18 square inches. Find the circumference of the circle to the nearest tenth of an inch. Use 3.14 for π.

    A. 2.4   C. 15.1

    B. 7.5   D. 30.1

3. What are the rays that intersect at point Y?

    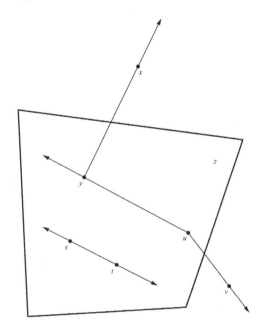

    A. $\overrightarrow{YX}$ and $\overrightarrow{UY}$ C. $\overrightarrow{XY}$ and $\overrightarrow{UY}$

    B. $\overrightarrow{YX}$ and $\overrightarrow{YU}$ D. $\overrightarrow{XY}$ and $\overrightarrow{YU}$

4. Select the drawing of $\overrightarrow{AB}$ and $\overrightarrow{CD}$ intersecting at D.

    A.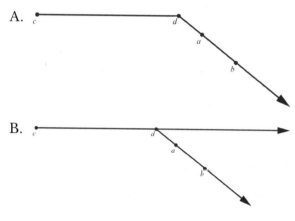

    B.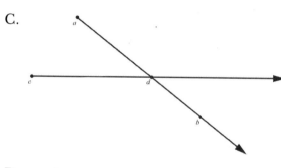

    C.

    D.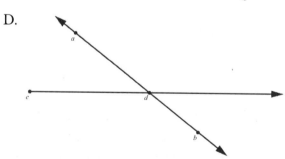

5. Which statement best describes the multiples of a whole number?

   A. The multiples of a whole number exclude 0.

   B. The multiples of a whole number are integers.

   C. The multiples of a whole number are all positive.

   D. The multiples of a whole number are all negative.

6. How many whole-number factors does a prime number have?

   A. 0

   B. 1

   C. 2

   D. Not enough information

7. A rectangular pyramid has a height of 7 meters and a volume of 112 cubic meters. Find the area of the base in square meters.

   A. 16

   B. 28

   C. 42

   D. 48

8. Find the volume in cubic centimeters of a square pyramid with a side length of 4 centimeters and a height of 12 centimeters.

   A. 48

   B. 64

   C. 144

   D. 192

9. A box in the shape of a right rectangular prism has dimensions of 6 centimeters by 7 centimeters by 8 centimeters. What is the volume in cubic centimeters?

   A. 280

   B. 336

   C. 560

   D. 672

10. A stop sign is a regular octagon with an area of 27,000 square centimeters and an apothem of 90 centimeters. What is the length in centimeters of one side?

    A. 38

    B. 75

    C. 300

    D. 600

11. Solve the equation by the quadratic formula, $x^2 + 10x + 8 = 0$.

    A. -0.88 and 9.13

    B. 0.88 and -9.13

    C. -0.88 and -9.13

    D. 0.88 and 9.13

12. Solve the equation by the square root method, $2x^2 = 162$.

    A. ± 8

    B. ± 9

    C. ± 10

    D. ± 11

CHAPTER 3 ADVANCED ALGEBRA AND GEOMETRY
PRACTICE QUIZ 1 – ANSWER KEY

1. A. The correct solution is 207.64 because $A = \frac{1}{2}(3.14r^2) = \frac{1}{2}(3.14r \times 11.5^2) = \frac{1}{2}(3.14 \times 132.25)$ $= \frac{1}{2}(415.265) \approx 207.64$ square feet. **See Lesson: Circles.**

2. C. The correct solution is 15.1.

$18 = 3.14r^2$; $5.73 = r^2$; $r \approx 2.4$ centimeters. $C = 2\pi r$; $C = 2(3.14)(2.4) \approx 15.1$ centimeters.

See Lesson: Circles.

3. A. The correct solution is $\overrightarrow{YX}$ and $\overrightarrow{UY}$ because these rays intersect at point Y. **See Lesson: Congruence.**

4. C. The correct solution is C. The two rays intersect at point D. **See Lesson: Congruence.**

5. B. Any product of a whole number and an integer is a multiple of that number. Note that the multiples of a whole number and another whole number must be integers because they are the products of two whole factors. Changing the sign of these products does not change their status as integers. Therefore, the multiples of a whole number are all integers. An alternative approach to this question is elimination: the products of 9 and 0, 1, and −1 are 0, 9, and −9; therefore, answers A, B, and C are false. **See Lesson: Factors and Multiples.**

6. C. Recall that a number is prime if it only has 1 and itself as factors. Both must be whole; therefore, a prime number has two whole-number factors. **See Lesson: Factors and Multiples.**

7. D. The correct solution is 48. Substitute the values into the formula, $112 = \frac{1}{3}B\left(7\right)$ and simplify the right side of the equation, $112 = \frac{7}{3}B$. Multiply both sides of the equation by the reciprocal, $B = 48$ square meters. **See Lesson: Measurement and Dimension.**

8. B. The correct solution is 64. Substitute the values into the formula and simplify using the order of operations, $V = \frac{1}{3}Bh = \frac{1}{3}s^2h = \frac{1}{3}(4^2)12 = \frac{1}{3}(16)(12) = 64$ cubic centimeters. **See Lesson: Measurement and Dimension.**

9. B. The correct solution is 336. Substitute the values into the formula and simplify using the order of operations, $V = lwh = 6(7)(8)$ cubic centimeters. **See Lesson: Similarity, Right Triangles, and Trigonometry.**

10. B. The correct solution is 75. Substitute the values into the formula, $27{,}000 = \frac{1}{2}(90)p$ and simplify using the order of operations, $27{,}000 = 45p$. Divide both sides of the equation by 45 to find the perimeter, $p = 600$ centimeters. Divide the perimeter by 8 to find the length of 75 centimeters for each side. **See Lesson: Similarity, Right Triangles, and Trigonometry.**

11. C. The correct solutions are -0.88 and -9.13. **See Lesson: Solving Quadratic Equations.**

$x = \dfrac{-10 \pm \sqrt{10^2 - 4(1)(8)}}{2(1)}$ Substitute 1 for a, 10 for b, and 8 for c.

$x = \dfrac{-10 \pm \sqrt{100 - 32}}{2}$ Apply the exponent and perform the multiplication.

$x = \dfrac{-10 \pm \sqrt{68}}{2}$ Perform the subtraction.

$x = \dfrac{-10 \pm 8.25}{2}$ Apply the square root.

$x = \dfrac{-10 + 8.25}{2}, \ x = \dfrac{-10 - 8.25}{2}$ Separate the problem into two expressions.

$x = \dfrac{-1.75}{2} = -0.88, \ x = \dfrac{-18.25}{2} = -9.13$ Simplify the numerator and divide.

12. B. The correct solution is ± 9. **See Lesson: Solving Quadratic Equations.**

$x^2 = 81$ Divide both sides of the equation by 2.

$x = \pm 9$ Apply the square root to both sides of the equation.

CHAPTER 3 ADVANCED ALGEBRA AND GEOMETRY
PRACTICE QUIZ 2

1. A half circle has an area of 50 square inches. Find the radius to the nearest tenth of an inch. Use 3.14 for π.

   A. 1.4   C. 4.2

   B. 2.8   D. 5.6

2. The bottom of a plastic pool has an area of 64 square feet. What is the radius to the nearest tenth of a foot? Use 3.14 for π.

   A. 2.3   C. 6.9

   B. 4.5   D. 10.2

3. What points in the diagram are collinear?

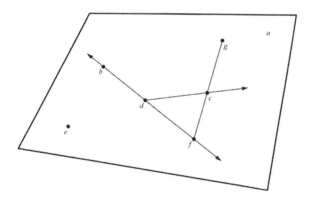

   A. Points D, C, and F

   B. Points B, D, and F

   C. Points B, C, and E

   D. Points B, C, and D

4. Name the right angle in the diagram.

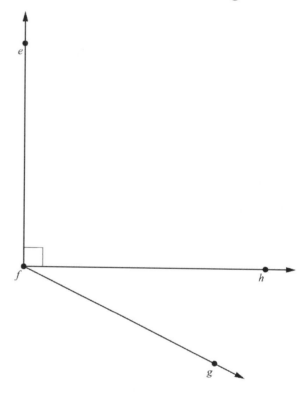

   A. ∠EHF   C. ∠EFH

   B. ∠EFG   D. ∠EGF

5. Which type of number is always composite?

   A. The product of two prime numbers

   B. The product of two whole numbers

   C. The product of 0 and a prime number

   D. The product of 1 and a whole number

6. How many unique prime factors does 75 have?

   A. 1   C. 3

   B. 2   D. 4

7. A jar of salsa has a diameter of 12 centimeters and a height of 10 centimeters. There are 4 centimeters of salsa left in the jar. How much salsa was used if the jar was originally filled to the top? State the answer in cubic centimeters in terms of π.

   A. 216π C. 864π

   B. 360π D. $1{,}440\pi$

8. A cone has a radius of 4 centimeters and a height of 9 centimeters. Find the volume in cubic centimeters.

   A. 16π C. 48π

   B. 32π D. 64π

9. Three vertices of a parallelogram are $(8,5)$, $(-2,5)$, $(-1,1)$. What is the fourth coordinate?

   A. $(9, 1)$ C. $(9, -1)$

   B. $(8, 1)$ D. $(8, -1)$

10. A cube has a surface area of 54 square feet. What is the side length in feet?

    A. 2   C. 4

    B. 3   D. 5

11. Solve the equation by any method, $x^2 + 16x + 33 = 0$.

    A. $-8 \pm \sqrt{31}$ C. $-8 \pm \sqrt{33}$

    B. $8 \pm \sqrt{31}$ D. $8 \pm \sqrt{33}$

12. Solve the equation by any method, $6x^2 + 19x + 10 = 0$.

    A. $\frac{5}{2}$ and $\frac{2}{3}$ C. $-\frac{5}{2}$ and $\frac{2}{3}$

    B. $\frac{5}{2}$ and $-\frac{2}{3}$ D. $-\frac{5}{2}$ and $-\frac{2}{3}$

Chapter 3 Advanced Algebra and Geometry
Practice Quiz 2 – Answer Key

1. D. The correct solution is 5.6 because $A = 12r^2$; $50 = (12)3.14r^2$; $50 = 1.57r^2$; $31.85 = r^2$; $r \approx 5.6$ inches. **See Lesson: Circles.**

2. B. The correct solution is 4.5 because $A = \pi r^2$; $64 = 3.14r^2$; $20.38 = r2$; $r \approx 4.5$ feet. **See Lesson: Circles.**

3. B. The correct solution is points B, D, and F because these points are line $\overleftrightarrow{BF}$. **See Lesson: Congruence.**

4. C. The correct solution is $\angle EFH$ because the vertex of the right angle is F and the other two points are E and H. **See Lesson: Congruence.**

5. A. The product of two prime numbers has those two prime numbers as factors, and because a prime number is greater than or equal to 2, the product must be at least 4. Therefore, its factors must include numbers other than itself and 1—specifically, the two prime numbers. **See Lesson: Factors and Multiples.**

6. B. The prime factorization—for example, using a factor tree—shows that 75 has the prime factors 3, 5, and 5, since $3 \times 5 \times 5 = 75$. Because 5 repeats, 75 has only two unique prime factors. **See Lesson: Factors and Multiples.**

7. A. The correct solution is 216π. The radius is one-half of the diameter, 6 centimeters. The height of the used salsa is $10 - 4$, or 6 centimeters. Substitute the values into the formula and simplify using the order of operations, $V = \pi r^2 h = \pi 6^2(6) = \pi(36)(6) = 216\pi$ cubic centimeters. **See Lesson: Measurement and Dimension.**

8. C. The correct solution is 48π cubic centimeters. Substitute the values into the formula and simplify using the order of operations, $V = \frac{1}{3}\pi r^2 h = \frac{1}{3}\pi(4^2)(9) = \frac{1}{3}\pi(16)(9) = 48\pi$ cubic centimeters. **See Lesson: Measurement and Dimension.**

9. A. The correct solution is $(9, 1)$ because this point shows a parallelogram with a base length of 10 units. **See Lesson: Similarity, Right Triangles, and Trigonometry.**

10. B. The correct solution is 3. Substitute the values into the formula $54 = 6s^2$. Solve the equation by dividing both sides of the equation by 6 and applying the square root, $9 = s^2; s = 3$ feet. **See Lesson: Similarity, Right Triangles, and Trigonometry.**

11. A. The correct solutions are $-8 \pm \sqrt{31}$. The equation can be solved by completing the square. **See Lesson: Solving Quadratic Equations.**

$x^2 + 16x = -33$	Subtract 33 from both sides of the equation.
$x^2 + 16x + 64 = -33 + 64$	Complete the square, $\left(\frac{16}{2}\right)^2 = 8^2 = 64$.
	Add 64 to both sides of the equation.
$x^2 + 16x + 64 = 31$	Simplify the right side of the equation.
$(x + 8)^2 = 31$	Factor the left side of the equation.
$x + 8 = \pm\sqrt{31}$	Apply the square root to both sides of the equation.
$x = -8 \pm \sqrt{31}$	Subtract 8 from both sides of the equation.

12. D. The correct solutions are $-\frac{5}{2}$ and $-\frac{2}{3}$. The equation can be solved by factoring. **See Lesson: Solving Quadratic Equations.**

$(2x + 5)(3x + 2) = 0$	Factor the equation.
$(2x + 5) = 0 \ (3x + 2) = 0$	Set each factor equal to 0.
$2x + 5 = 0$	Subtract 5 from both sides of the equation and divide both sides of the equation by 2 to solve.
$2x = -5$	
$x = -\frac{5}{2}$	
$3x + 2 = 0$	Subtract 2 from both sides of the equation and divide both sides of the equation by 3 to solve.
$3x = -2$	
$x = -\frac{2}{3}$	

SECTION II
FULL-LENGTH PRACTICE EXAMS

ACCUPLACER MATH PRACTICE EXAM 1

SECTION I. ARITHMETIC

1. What is the difference between natural numbers and whole numbers?

   A. They are the same.

   B. The whole numbers include zero, but the natural numbers exclude zero.

   C. The natural numbers only go to 10, but the whole numbers have no limit.

   D. The whole numbers include negative numbers, but the natural numbers do not.

2. Evaluate the expression 1,004 + 110.

   A. 2,104   C. 1,204

   B. 1,411   D. 1,114

3. Which statement is true?

   A. A numeral is a symbol that represents a number.

   B. A number is a symbol that represents a numeral.

   C. Numerals and numbers are the same.

   D. None of the above.

4. Which statement best describes a remainder in division?

   A. The quotient minus the divisor

   B. The product of the dividend and divisor

   C. The difference between the dividend and the quotient

   D. The portion of a dividend not evenly divisible by the divisor

5. Evaluate the expression $15 \times (-15)$.

   A. -225 C. -1

   B. -30 D. 0

6. What is $762 \div 127$?

   A. 4   C. 8

   B. 6   D. 9

7. Which decimal is the greatest?

   A. 1.7805   C. 1.7085

   B. 1.5807   D. 1.8057

8. Change $0.\overline{63}$ to a fraction. Simplify completely.

   A. $\frac{5}{9}$ C. $\frac{2}{3}$

   B. $\frac{7}{11}$ D. $\frac{5}{6}$

9. Write $0.\overline{1}$ as a percent.

   A. $0.\overline{1}\%$ C. $11.\overline{1}\%$

   B. $1.\overline{1}\%$ D. $111.\overline{1}\%$

10. Write $83.\overline{3}\%$ as a decimal.

    A. $8.\overline{3}$ C. $0.08\overline{3}$

    B. $0.8\overline{3}$ D. 0.0083

11. **Two companies have made a chart of paid time off. Which statement describes the mean and standard deviation?**

Paid Time off for Employees at Company A

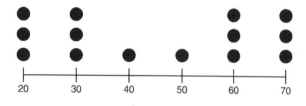

Paid Time off for Employees at Company B

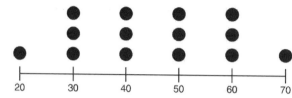

A. The means are the same, but the standard deviation is smaller for Company B.

B. The means are the same, but the standard deviation is smaller for Company A.

C. The mean is greater for Company A, and the standard deviation is smaller for Company A.

D. The mean is greater for Company B, and the standard deviation is smaller for Company B.

12. **Find the values from the box plot.**

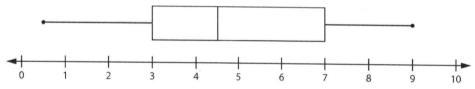

A. Minimum: 0, first quartile: 3, median: 5, third quartile: 7, maximum: 9

B. Minimum: 0.5, first quartile: 3, median: 4.5, third quartile: 7, maximum: 9

C. Minimum: 0, first quartile: 3, median: 5, third quartile: 7, maximum: 10

D. Minimum: 0.5, first quartile: 3, median: 4.5, third quartile: 7, maximum: 10

13. The data below shows a class's quiz scores out of 20 points.

5, 5, 6, 7, 8, 8, 9, 10, 11, 12, 13, 14, 15, 15, 16, 18, 18, 19, 20, 20

Select a box plot for the data.

A.
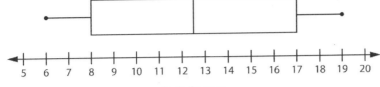

B.
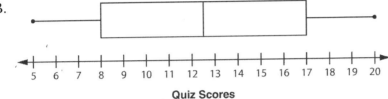

C.

D.
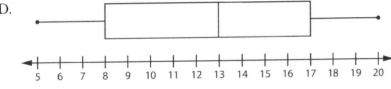

14. Divide $1\frac{2}{3} \div 3\frac{7}{12}$.

   A. $\frac{20}{43}$ C. $3\frac{3}{4}$

   B. $3\frac{7}{18}$ D. $5\frac{35}{36}$

15. Multiply $\frac{4}{5} \times \frac{1}{5}$.

   A. $\frac{4}{25}$ C. $\frac{3}{5}$

   B. $\frac{2}{5}$ D. $\frac{16}{25}$

16. Divide $8 \div \frac{2}{9}$.

   A. 9   C. 36

   B. 18   D. 72

17. Multiply $\frac{2}{5} \times 3$.

   A. $\frac{2}{15}$ C. $2\frac{3}{5}$

   B. $1\frac{1}{5}$ D. $3\frac{2}{5}$

18. Which is different from the others?

   A. 6.4%

   B. $\frac{8}{125}$

   C. 128:2000

   D. All of the above are equal.

19. Which proportion yields a number for the unknown that is different from the others?

   A. $\frac{13}{75} = \frac{158}{?}$ C. $\frac{158}{?} = \frac{13}{75}$

   B. $\frac{75}{13} = \frac{?}{158}$ D. $\frac{75}{13} = \frac{158}{?}$

20. The number 22 is what percent of 54?

   A. 22%   C. 41%

   B. 29%   D. 76%

SECTION II. QUANTITATIVE REASONING, ALGEBRA, AND STATISTICS

1. Solve the equation for the unknown, $\frac{c}{-4} = -12$.

   A. −16

   B. −8

   C. 3

   D. 48

2. Solve the inequality for the unknown, $3(x + 1) + 2(x + 1) \geq 5(3-x) + 4(x + 2)$.

   A. $x \geq 0$

   B. $x \geq 1$

   C. $x \geq 2$

   D. $x \geq 3$

3. Solve the system of equations,
   $$2y + x = -20$$
   $$y = -x-12$$

   A. (4, 8)

   B. (4, -8)

   C. (-4, 8)

   D. (-4, -8)

4. Solve the system of equations by graphing,
   $$3x + y = -1$$
   $$2x-y = -4$$

   A.

   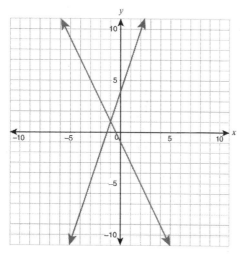

B.

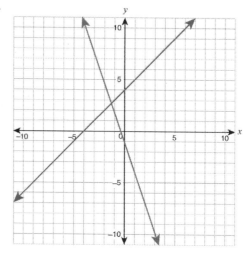

C.

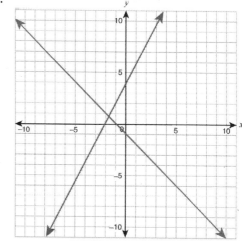

D.

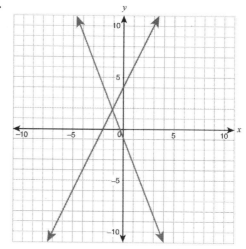

5. Solve the system of equations,

$$y = x$$
$$x^2 + y^2 = 10.$$

A. (3, 3) and (-3, -3)

B. (3, -3) and (-3, 3)

C. (2.2, 2.2) and (-2.2, -2.2)

D. (2.2, -2.2) and (-2.2, 2.2)

6. Find the median for the data set 34, 31, 37, 35, 38, 33, 39, 32, 36, 35, 37, and 33.

A. 34   C. 36

B. 35   D. 37

7. The bar chart shows the number of items collected for a charity drive. What is the total number of items collected for the three highest classes?

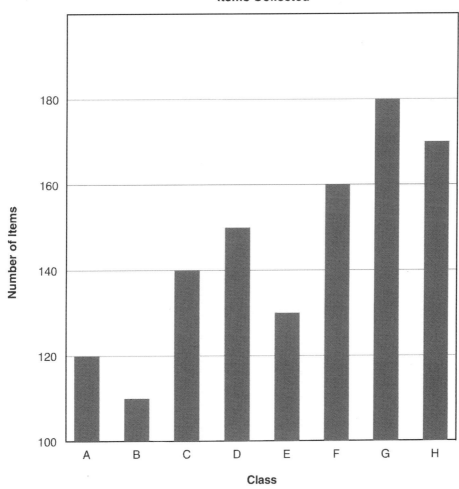

Items Collected

A. 500   C. 520

B. 510   D. 530

8. The table shows the speed in miles per hour of different roller coasters at an amusement park. Select the correct line graph for this data.

Amusement Park Roller Coasters	1	2	3	4	5	6	7	8
Speed (miles per hour)	120	105	75	100	60	85	110	90

A.

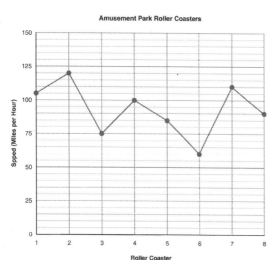

C.

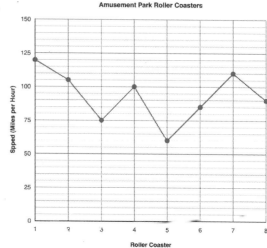

B.

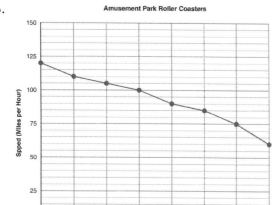

D.

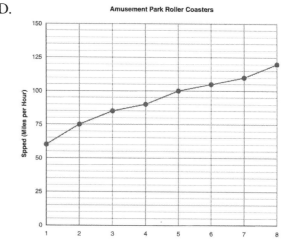

9. Multiply, $(5x–3)(5x + 3)$.

A. $25x^2–9$

B. $25x^2 + 9$

C. $25x^2 + 30x–9$

D. $25x^2 + 30x + 9$

10. Perform the operation,
$(-3x^2–2xy + 4y^2) + (5x^2 + 3xy–3y^2)$.

A. $2x^2–xy + y^2$

B. $–2x^2–xy + y^2$

C. $–2x^2 + xy + y^2$

D. $2x^2 + xy + y^2$

11. Apply the polynomial identity to rewrite $x^3 + 125$.

A. $(x + 5)(x^2–5x + 25)$

B. $(x–5)(x^2–10x + 25)$

C. $(x + 5)(x^2 + 5x + 25)$

D. $(x–5)(x^2 + 10x + 25)$

124

12. Simplify $\left(\dfrac{x^3 y^{-2}}{x^{-2} y^3}\right)^5$.

   A. $\dfrac{1}{x^{25} y^{25}}$

   B. $\dfrac{y^{25}}{x^{25}}$

   C. $\dfrac{x^{25}}{y^{25}}$

   D. $x^{25} y^{25}$

13. One athlete had a salary of about 3×10^7 dollars per year and another athlete had a salary of about 2×10^6 dollars per year. How many times larger is the salary of the first athlete?

   A. 2

   B. 5

   C. 10

   D. 15

14. Solve $x^3 = -216$.

   A. –6

   B. –4

   C. 4

   D. 6

15. There is an election at a school where 4 candidates out of 10 will be elected. Which object and results are the most appropriate for a simulation?

   A. Toss a coin

   B. Ten-sided number cube and use multiples of 2

   C. Eight-section spinner and use the odd numbers

   D. Throw two six-sided number cubes and use the results of 1 and 6

16. A study looked at a random sample of people and watched their use of social media on mobile devices. The researcher looked at which group of users were happier. What type of study is this?

   A. Census

   B. Survey

   C. Experiment

   D. Observational study

17. A doctor wants to study the effects of a low-fat diet in patients. What would be needed to create an observational study?

   A. Ask how many fat calories were eaten and track weight.

   B. Ask about the amount of weight patients have gained or lost.

   C. Have one-half of the patients eat a high-fat diet and the other eat a low-fat diet.

   D. Select a group of patients with a low-fat diet and ask how they feel being on the diet.

18. A bag contains 10 red marbles, 8 black marbles, and 7 white marbles. What is the probability of selecting a black marble first and a red marble second with no replacement?

   A. $\dfrac{8}{25}$

   B. $\dfrac{16}{125}$

   C. $\dfrac{2}{15}$

   D. $\dfrac{7}{75}$

19. Which option results in the greatest gain on an investment?

   A. 100% of gaining $1,000

   B. 60% of gaining $2,500 and 40% of gaining $0

   C. 75% of gaining $1,000 and 25% of gaining $1,500

   D. 70% of gaining $1,500 and 30% of gaining $1,000

20. In a deck of 20 number cards, cards 1–5 are green, cards 6–10 are red, cards 11–15 are yellow, and cards 16–20 are blue. Describe the complement of even cards.

   A. Odd number cards

   B. Even number cards

   C. Green and red cards

   D. Yellow and blue cards

SECTION III. ADVANCED ALGEBRA AND FUNCTIONS

1. A circular dinner plate has a diameter of 13 inches. A ring is placed along the edge of the plate. Find the circumference of the ring in inches. Use 3.14 for π.

   A. 31.4

   B. 40.82

   C. 62.8

   D. 81.64

2. Identify the diameter of the circle.

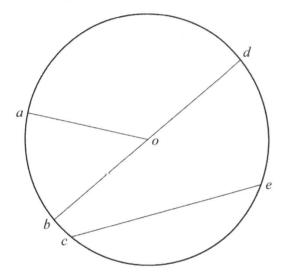

   A. $\overline{AO}$

   C. $\overline{CE}$

   B. $\overline{BD}$

   D. $\overline{AC}$

3. A circle has a circumference of 72 centimeters. Find the radius to the nearest tenth of a centimeter. Use 3.14 for π.

   A. 6.3

   C. 17.2

   B. 11.5

   D. 22.9

4. The circumference of a pie is 300 centimeters. Find the area of one-fourth of the pie to the nearest tenth of a square centimeter. Use 3.14 for π.

   A. 1,793.6

   C. 7,174.4

   B. 2,284.8

   D. 14,348.8

5. What is the order of rotational symmetry for a parallelogram?

   A. 1

   C. 3

   B. 2

   D. 4

6. Select the square with the correct lines of symmetry.

   A.

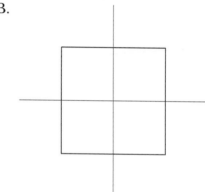

   B.

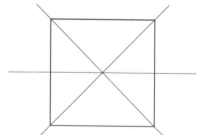

   C.

   D.

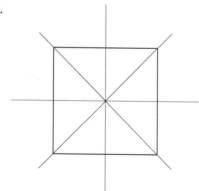

7. Identify the coplanar points in the diagram.

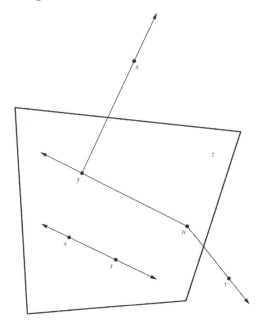

A. Points S, T, U, and Y

B. Points X, V, S, and Z

C. Points X, Y, U, and V

D. Points U, Y, Z, and T

8. If the term of a mobile-phone contract is in multiples of a year, which duration can a customer choose?

A. 6 months
C. 24 months

B. 18 months
D. 32 months

9. Which number is a factor of 128?

A. 3
C. 12

B. 6
D. 16

10. What are the unique prime factors of 56?

A. 2, 7
C. 2, 5, 7

B. 1, 2, 7
D. 2, 4, 7, 8, 14, 16, 28

11. A rectangular pyramid has a length of 10 centimeters, a width of 11 inches, and a height of 12 inches. Find the volume in cubic inches.

A. 220
C. 660

B. 440
D. 880

12. A cylinder has an outer radius of 6 inches. There is a hole cut out of the center with a radius of 4 inches. The volume of the solid part is 260π cubic inches. Find the height of the cylinder.

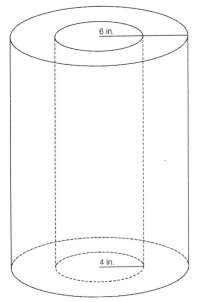

A. 2 inches
C. 13 inches

B. 9 inches
D. 26 inches

13. A sphere has a volume of 972π cubic millimeters. Find the radius in millimeters.

A. 3
C. 27

B. 9
D. 81

14. A square pyramid has a volume of 189 cubic feet and a height of 7 feet. Find the length in feet of a side of the base.

A. 3
C. 12

B. 9
D. 18

15. A regular hexagon has a side length of 5 inches and an apothem of 2 inches. Find the area in square inches.

    A. 30   C. 50

    B. 40   D. 60

16. Given the coordinates for a rectangle $(-4,-1), (-9,-1), (-9,-8), (-4,-8)$, find the length of each side of the rectangle.

    A. 2 units and 3 units   C. 5 units and 3 units

    B. 2 units and 7 units   D. 5 units and 7 units

17. Three vertices of a rectangle are $(-6, 5), (-6, 0), (12, 5)$.
    What is the fourth coordinate?

    A. $(12, 0)$ C. $(-12, 0)$

    B. $(0, 12)$ D. $(0, -12)$

18. Solve the equation by any method, $x^2 - 23x + 125 = 0$.

    A. -8.81 and -14.2 C. 8.81 and -14.2

    B. 8.81 and 14.2 D. -8.81 and 14.2

19. Solve the equation by factoring, $x^2 + 3x - 88 = 0$.

    A. $-8, -11$ C. $8, -11$

    B. $-8, 11$ D. $8, 11$

20. Solve the equation by the quadratic formula, $12x^2 + x - 3 = 0$.

    A. -0.46 and -0.54

    B. 0.46 and -0.54

    C. -0.46 and 0.54

    D. 0.46 and 0.54

ACCUPLACER MATH PRACTICE EXAM 1
ANSWER KEY WITH EXPLANATORY ANSWERS

Section I. Arithmetic

1. B. The correct solution is the whole numbers include zero, but the natural numbers exclude zero. The natural or "counting" numbers are 1, 2, 3, 4,.... To get the whole numbers, just include 0 with the natural numbers. **See Lesson: Basic Addition and Subtraction.**

2. D. The correct solution is 1,114. Use the addition algorithm or note the two numbers never have nonzero digits in the same place. This fact allows addition by inspection. **See Lesson: Basic Addition and Subtraction.**

3. A. The correct solution is a numeral is a symbol that represents a number. Recall that numbers are abstract quantities, but a numeral is a symbol that represents a number. **See Lesson: Basic Addition and Subtraction.**

4. D. When dividing whole numbers, the remainder is the portion of the dividend left over after finding the whole-number part of the quotient. The remainder is always smaller than the divisor. **See Lesson: Basic Multiplication and Division.**

5. A. When multiplying signed numbers, remember that the product of a negative and a positive is negative. Other than the sign, the process is the same as multiplying whole numbers. **See Lesson: Basic Multiplication and Division.**

6. B. Use the division algorithm. Because 127 is greater than 7 and 76, the process begins with all three digits in the dividend. **See Lesson: Basic Multiplication and Division.**

7. D. The correct solution is 1.8057 because 1.8057 contains the largest value in the tenths place. **See Lesson: Decimals and Fractions.**

8. B. The correct solution is $\frac{7}{11}$. Let $n = 0.\overline{63}$ and $100n = 63.\overline{63}$ Then, $100n - n = 63.\overline{63} - 0.\overline{63}$ resulting in $99n = 63$ and solution of $n = \frac{63}{99} = \frac{7}{11}$. **See Lesson: Decimals and Fractions.**

9. C. The correct answer is $11.\overline{1}\%$ because $0.\overline{1}$ as a percent is $0.\overline{1} \times 100 = 11.\overline{1}\%$. **See Lesson: Decimals and Fractions.**

10. B. The correct answer is $0.8\overline{3}$ because $83.\overline{3}\%$ as a decimal is $0.8\overline{3}$. **See Lesson: Decimals and Fractions.**

11. A. The correct solution is the means are the same, but the standard deviation is greater for Company B. The standard deviation is smaller for Company B because more values are closer to the mean. **See Lesson: Interpreting Categorical and Quantitative Data.**

12. B. The correct solution is minimum: 0.5, first quartile: 3, median: 4.5, third quartile: 7, maximum: 9, which are the values of the box plot. **See Lesson: Interpreting Categorical and Quantitative Data.**

13. B. The correct response is B. The median value is 12.5, the first quartile value is 8, and the third quartile value is 17. The minimum is 5, and the maximum is 20. **See Lesson: Interpreting Categorical and Quantitative Data.**

14. A. The correct answer is $\frac{20}{43}$ because $\frac{5}{3} \div \frac{43}{12} = \frac{5}{3} \times \frac{12}{43} = \frac{60}{129} = \frac{20}{43}$. **See Lesson: Multiplication and Division of Fractions.**

15. A. The correct solution is $\frac{4}{25}$ because $\frac{4}{5} \times \frac{1}{5} = \frac{4}{25}$. **See Lesson: Multiplication and Division of Fractions.**

16. C. 36 is the correct answer because $\frac{8}{1} \times \frac{9}{2} = \frac{72}{2} = 36$. **See Lesson: Multiplication and Division of Fractions.**

17. B. The correct solution is $1\frac{1}{5}$ because $\frac{2}{5} \times \frac{3}{1} = \frac{6}{5} = 1\frac{1}{5}$. **See Lesson: Multiplication and Division of Fractions.**

18. D. All of the answer choices are equal. Although answer C is not in lowest terms, it is equal to $\frac{8}{125}$, which is equal to 0.064 or 6.4%. **See Lesson: Ratios, Proportions, and Percentages.**

19. D. The correct answer is D. Although solving each proportion is one approach, the easiest approach is to compare them as they are. The proportions in answers A and B yield the same number for the unknown because they keep the same numbers in either the numerators or the denominators. Answer C just reverses the order of the equation in answer A, which does not yield a different number for the unknown. Answer D flips one fraction without flipping the other, which changes the proportion. **See Lesson: Ratios, Proportions, and Percentages.**

20. C. The fraction $\frac{22}{54}$ is 41%, meaning 22 is 41% of 54. **See Lesson: Ratios, Proportions, and Percentages.**

Section II. Quantitative Reasoning, Algebra, and Statistics

1. D. The correct solution is 48 because both sides of the equation are multiplied by -4. **See Lesson: Equations with One Variable.**

2. D. The correct solution is $x \geq 3$.

$3x + 3 + 2x + 2 \geq 15 - 5x + 4x + 8$	Apply the distributive property.
$5x + 5 \geq -x + 23$	Combine like terms on both sides of the inequality.
$6x + 5 \geq 23$	Add x to both sides of the inequality.
$6x \geq 18$	Subtract 5 from both sides of the inequality.
$x \geq 3$	Divide both sides of the inequality by 6.

See Lesson: Equations with One Variable.

3. D. The correct solution is (-4, -8).

	The second equation is already solved for y.
$2(-x-12) + x = -20$	Substitute $-x-12$ in for y in the first equation.
$-2x-24 + x = -20$	Apply the distributive property.
$-x-24 = -20$	Combine like terms on the left side of the equation.
$-x = 4$	Add 24 to both sides of the equation.
$x = -4$	Divide both sides of the equation by -1.
$y = -(-4)-12$	Substitute -4 in the second equation for x.
$y = 4-12 = -8$	Simplify using order of operations.

See Lesson: Equations with Two Variables.

4. D. The correct graph has the two lines intersect at (-1, 2). **See Lesson: Equations with Two Variables.**

5. C. The correct solutions are (2.2, 2.2) and (-2.2, -2.2).

$x^2 + x^2 = 10$	Substitute x in for y in the second equation.
$2x^2 = 10$	Combine like terms on the left side of the equation.
$x^2 = 5$	Divide both sides of the equation by 2.
$x = \pm 2.2$	Apply the square root to both sides of the equation.
$y = 2.2$	Substitute 2.2 in the first equation.
$y = -2.2$	Substitute -2.2 in the first equation.

See Lesson: Equations with Two Variables.

6. B. The correct solution is 35. The data set in order is 31, 32, 33, 33, 34, 35, 35, 36, 37, 37, 38, 39, and the middle numbers are both 35. Therefore, the median is 35. **See Lesson: Interpreting Graphics.**

7. B. The correct solution is 510 items because the three largest classes collected 180, 170, and 160 items. **See Lesson: Interpreting Graphics.**

8. C. The correct solution is C. The line graph has the correct values for each roller coaster. **See Lesson: Interpreting Graphics.**

9. A. The correct solution is $25x^2-9$.

$$(5x-3)(5x + 3) = 5x(5x + 3)-3(5x + 3) = 25x^2 + 15x-15x-9 = 25x^2-9$$

See Lesson: Polynomials.

10. D. The correct solution is $2x^2 + xy + y^2$.

$$(-3x^2-2xy + 4y^2) + (5x^2 + 3xy-3y^2) = (-3x^2 + 5x^2) + (-2xy + 3xy) + (4y^2-3y^2) = 2x^2 + xy + y^2$$

See Lesson: Polynomials.

11. A. The correct solution is $(x + 5)(x^2 - 5x + 25)$. The expression $x^3 + 125$ is rewritten as $(x + 5)(x^2 - 5x + 25)$ because the value of a is x and the value of b is 5. **See Lesson: Polynomials.**

12. C. The correct solution is $\frac{x^{25}}{y^{25}}$ because $\left(\frac{x^3 y^{-2}}{x^{-2} y^3}\right)^5 = \left(x^{3-(-2)} y^{-2-3}\right)^5 = \left(x^5 y^{-5}\right)^5 = x^{5 \times 5} y^{-5 \times 5} = x^{25} y^{-25} = \frac{x^{25}}{y^{25}}$. **See Lesson: Powers, Exponents, Roots, and Radicals.**

13. D. The correct solution is 15 because the first athlete's salary is about \$30,000,000 and the second athlete's salary is about \$2,000,000. So, the first athlete's salary is about 15 times larger. **See Lesson: Powers, Exponents, Roots, and Radicals.**

14. A. The correct solution is –6 because the cube root of –216 is –6. **See Lesson: Powers, Exponents, Roots, and Radicals.**

15. B. The correct solution is ten-sided number cube and use multiples of 2 because there are 4 results out of 10 that would match the probability of the actual event. **See Lesson: Statistical Measures.**

16. D. The correct solution is observational study because people were not randomly assigned to group and their behaviors were observed. **See Lesson: Statistical Measures.**

17. A. The correct solution is to ask how many fat calories patients eat and track patients' weight because the researcher is observing the number of fat calories eaten and the weight. **See Lesson: Statistical Measures.**

18. C. The correct solution is $\frac{2}{15}$. There are 8 marbles out of 25 for the first event and 10 marbles out of 24 for the second event. The probability of the event is $\frac{8}{25} \times \frac{10}{24} = \frac{80}{600} = \frac{2}{15}$. **See Lesson: Statistics & Probability: The Rules of Probability.**

19. B. The correct solution is 60% of gaining \$2,500 and 40% of gaining \$0. The expected value is $0.60(2,500) + 0.40(0) = \$1,500$. **See Lesson: Statistics & Probability: The Rules of Probability.**

20. A. The correct solution is odd number cards. The complement of even number cards is odd. **See Lesson: Statistics & Probability: The Rules of Probability.**

Section III. Advanced Algebra and Functions

1. B. The correct solution is 40.82 because $C = \pi d \approx 3.14(13) \approx 40.82$ inches. **See Lesson: Circles.**

2. B. The correct solution is $\overline{BD}$ because B and D are on the circle and the segment goes through the center of the circle. **See Lesson: Circles.**

3. B. The correct solution is 11.5 centimeters because $C = 2\pi r; 72 = (2)3.14r; 72 = 6.28r; r \approx 11.5$ centimeters. **See Lesson: Circles.**

4. A. The correct solution is 1,793.6. $C = 2\pi r; 300 = 2(3.14)r; 300 = 6.28r; r \approx 47.8$ centimeters. $A = \frac{1}{4}\pi r^2 \approx \frac{1}{4}(3.14)(47.8)^2 \approx \frac{1}{4}3.14(2,284.84) \approx 1793.6$ square centimeters. **See Lesson: Circles.**

5. B. The correct solution is 2. For a parallelogram, there is rotational symmetry every 180°. **See Lesson: Congruence.**

6. D. The correct solution is the square with four lines of symmetry. There is a horizontal line, a vertical line, and two diagonals of symmetry that map the rectangle onto itself. **See Lesson: Congruence.**

7. A. The correct solution is points *S, T, U,* and *Y* because these four points are in plane *Z*. **See Lesson: Congruence.**

8. C. A year-long contract is also 12 months long. Multiples of 12 months are 24 months, 36 months, 48 months, and so on. **See Lesson: Factors and Multiples.**

9. D. To determine whether a number is a factor of another number, divide the second number by the first number. If the quotient is whole, the first number is a factor. In this case, 128 is only divisible by 16. **See Lesson: Factors and Multiples.**

10. A. The prime factorization of 56—for example, using a factor tree—yields the numbers 2, 2, 2, and 7. Ignoring repeats of 2, the unique prime factors are 2 and 7. **See Lesson: Factors and Multiples.**

11. B. The correct solution is 440. Substitute the values into the formula and simplify using the order of operations, $V = \frac{1}{3}Bh = \frac{1}{3}lwh = \frac{1}{3}(10)(11)12 = 440$ cubic inches. **See Lesson: Measurement and Dimension.**

12. C. The correct solution is 13 inches. Substitute the values into the formula, $260\pi = \pi 6^2 h - \pi 4^2 h$. Apply the exponent and combine like terms, $260\pi = \pi 36h - \pi 16h; 260\pi = 20\pi h$. Divide both sides of the equation by 20π, $h = 13$ inches. **See Lesson: Measurement and Dimension.**

13. B. The correct solution is 9 millimeters. Substitute the values into the formula, $972\pi = \frac{4}{3}\pi r^3$, then multiply by the reciprocal, $729 = r^3$, and apply the cube root, r = 9 millimeters. **See Lesson: Measurement and Dimension.**

14. B. The correct solution is 9. Substitute the values into the formula, $189 = \frac{1}{3}s^2(7)$ and simplify the right side of the equation, $189 = \frac{7}{3}s^2$. Multiply both sides by the reciprocal and apply the square root, $81 = s^2, s = 9$ feet. **See Lesson: Measurement and Dimension.**

15. A. The correct solution is 30. Substitute the values into the formula and simplify using the order of operations, $A = \frac{1}{2}ap = \frac{1}{2}(2)(6(5)) = 30$ square inches. **See Lesson: Similarity, Right Triangles, and Trigonometry.**

16. D. The correct solution is 5 units and 7 units. The difference between the *x*-coordinates is –4–(–9) = 5 units, and the difference between the *y*-coordinates is –1–(–8) = 7 units. **See Lesson: Similarity, Right Triangles, and Trigonometry.**

17. A. The correct solution is (12, 0) because this point shows a rectangle with sides lengths of 5 units and 18 units. **See Lesson: Similarity, Right Triangles, and Trigonometry.**

18. B. The correct solutions are 8.81 and 14.2. The equation can be solved by the quadratic formula.

$x = \dfrac{-(-23) \pm \sqrt{(-23)^2 - 4(1)(125)}}{2(1)}$ Substitute 1 for a, –23 for b, and 125 for c.

$x = \dfrac{23 \pm \sqrt{529 - 500}}{2}$ Apply the exponent and perform the multiplication.

$x = \dfrac{23 \pm \sqrt{29}}{2}$ Perform the subtraction.

$x = \dfrac{23 \pm 5.39}{2}$ Apply the square root.

$x = \dfrac{23 + 5.39}{2}$, $x = \dfrac{23 - 5.39}{2}$ Separate the problem into two expressions.

$x = \dfrac{28.39}{2} = 14.2$, $x = \dfrac{17.61}{2} = 8.81$ Simplify the numerator and divide.

See Lesson: Solving Quadratic Equations.

19. C. The correct solutions are 8 and –11.

$(x + 11)(x - 8) = 0$ Factor the equation.

$(x + 11) = 0$ or $(x - 8) = 0$ Set each factor equal to 0.

$x + 11 = 0$ Subtract 11 from both sides of the equation to solve for the first factor.

$x = -11$

$x - 8 = 0$ Add 8 to both sides of the equation to solve for the second factor.

$x = 8$

See Lesson: Solving Quadratic Equations.

20. B. The correct solutions are 0.46 and −0.54.

$x = \dfrac{-1 \pm \sqrt{1^2 - 4(12)(-3)}}{2(12)}$ Substitute 12 ifor a, 1 for b, and −3 for c.

$x = \dfrac{-1 \pm \sqrt{1 - (-144)}}{24}$ Apply the exponent and perform the multiplication.

$x = \dfrac{-1 \pm \sqrt{145}}{24}$ Perform the subtraction.

$x = \dfrac{-1 \pm 12.04}{24}$ Apply the square root.

$x = \dfrac{-1 + 12.04}{24}$, $x = \dfrac{-1 - 12.04}{24}$ Separate the problem into two expressions.

$x = \dfrac{11.04}{24} = 0.46$, $x = \dfrac{-13.04}{24} = -0.54$ Simplify the numerator and divide.

See Lesson: Solving Quadratic Equations.

ACCUPLACER MATH PRACTICE EXAM 2

SECTION I. ARITHMETIC

1. Which procedure is impossible?

   A. Adding two negative numbers

   B. Subtracting a negative number from zero

   C. Adding two quantities with different units

   D. Placing negative numbers on the number line

2. How many millimeters are in a measurement that is 4 centimeters, 3 meters, and 7 millimeters long? (Note that a centimeter is 10 millimeters and a meter is 1,000 millimeters.)

   A. 347

   B. 437

   C. 3,047

   D. 3,407

3. What is 1,078 + 0?

   A. 1,078

   B. 1,079

   C. 2,156

   D. None of the above

4. Evaluate the expression 2,904 − 1,867.

   A. 1,037

   B. 1,867

   C. 4,771

   D. 5,000

5. Evaluate the expression 26 ÷ 9.

   A. 2

   B. 2R8

   C. 3R1

   D. 35

6. Which statement about multiplication is true?

   A. Multiplication is impossible.

   B. Multiplication is repeated division.

   C. Multiplication is repeated addition.

   D. Multiplication is repeated subtraction.

7. Evaluate the expression $(-20) \div (-5)$.

   A. −5

   B. −4

   C. 4

   D. 5

8. Each section of a science class has 36 slots, and each section must be full to be assigned a professor. If 203 students try to sign up, how many will not receive a slot?

   A. 1

   B. 3

   C. 23

   D. 36

9. Which decimal is the least?

   A. 2.22

   B. 2.02

   C. 2.002

   D. 2.2

10. Change 0.375 to a fraction. Simplify completely.

    A. $\frac{3}{8}$

    B. $\frac{2}{5}$

    C. $\frac{1}{2}$

    D. $\frac{7}{16}$

11. Write $\frac{1}{5}$ as a percent.

    A. 15%

    B. 20%

    C. 25%

    D. 30%

12. The test scores in a class are 82, 83, 84, 84, 85, 86, 88, 89, 90. The last test is a score of 105. Compare the mean and median before and after the last test score is included.

    A. The mean and median increase.

    B. The mean and median decrease.

    C. The mean increases, and the median does not change.

    D. The mean decreases, and the median does not change.

13. The last 8 transactions at a shoe store in dollars are 5, 39, 49, 50, 52, 35, 44, 100. What is the effect of removing the outliers on the mean and median?

   A. The mean and median increase.

   B. There is no effect on the mean or median.

   C. The mean decreases, but the median does not change.

   D. The median decreases, but the mean does not change.

14. Two companies have made a chart of paid time off. Which statement describes the median and interquartile range?

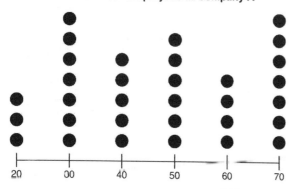
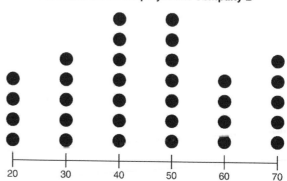

   A. The median is greater for Company A, and the interquartile range is greater for Company A.

   B. The median is greater for Company B, and the interquartile range is greater for Company B.

   C. The median is greater for Company A, but the interquartile range is greater for Company B.

   D. The median is greater for Company B, but the interquartile range is greater for Company A.

15. Divide $\frac{3}{4} \div \frac{1}{2}$.

   A. $\frac{1}{4}$

   B. $\frac{3}{8}$

   C. $1\frac{1}{5}$

   D. $1\frac{1}{2}$

16. Multiply $\frac{2}{3} \times \frac{4}{15}$.

   A. $\frac{3}{20}$

   B. $\frac{1}{6}$

   C. $\frac{8}{45}$

   D. $\frac{1}{3}$

17. Divide $2\frac{9}{10} \div 3\frac{1}{2}$.

   A. $\frac{2}{7}$

   B. $\frac{9}{20}$

   C. $\frac{2}{3}$

   D. $\frac{29}{35}$

18. Which is different from the others?

   A. 0.5

   B. 1:2

   C. $\frac{1}{2}$

   D. 1:2 odds

19. Which cannot be equal to the others?

   A. Ratio

   B. Fraction

   C. Percent

   D. Proportion

20. How many men does a company employ if it has 420 employees and 35% are women?

   A. 35

   B. 147

   C. 273

   D. 420

Section II. Quantitative Reasoning, Algebra, and Statistics

1. Solve the equation for the unknown,
   $a-10 = -20$.

   A. −30

   B. −10

   C. 2

   D. 200

2. Solve the inequality for the unknown,
   $\frac{2}{3}x-4 \leq \frac{4}{5}x + 2$.

   A. $x \leq -45$

   B. $x \geq -45$

   C. $x \leq 90$

   D. $x \geq 90$

3. Solve the equation for c, $2a(b + c) = c$.

   A. $\frac{2ab}{1-2a} = c$

   B. $\frac{2ab}{1 + 2a} = c$

   C. $\frac{2ab}{2a} = c$

   D. $\frac{2ab}{a} = c$

4. Solve the system of equations,

   $-2x + 6y = -6$
   $4x-5y = 26$.

   A. (2, 3)

   B. (3, 6)

   C. (6, 9)

   D. (9, 2)

5. Solve the system of equations by graphing,

   $y = -x + 7$
   $y = 2x-8$.

   A.

   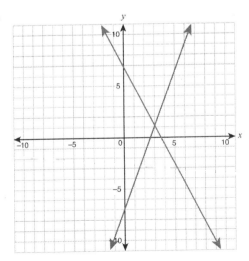

B.

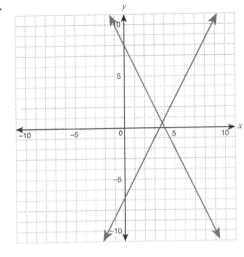

C.

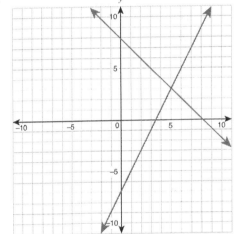

D.

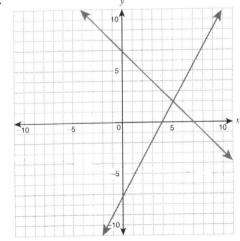

137

6. The data set represents the number of weekly pop-up ads for 12 families: 125, 145, 150, 130, 150, 120, 170, 165, 175, 145, 150, and 130. Find the median.

   A. 145
   B. 145.5
   C. 147
   D. 147.5

7. Find the mode for the data set 42, 45, 44, 44, 45, 42, 45, 44, 45, 46, 42, 44, 41, 48, 47, 46, 45, 42, 42, and 44.

   A. 42, 43
   B. 44, 45
   C. 42, 44, 45
   D. 42, 43, 44, 45

8. Find the mean for the data set 16, 18, 17, 15, 19, 14, 12, 11, 10, 16, 18, and 17.

   A. 14.25
   B. 15.25
   C. 16
   D. 17

9. Multiply, $(4x + 5)(3x-2)$.

   A. $12x^2-7x + 10$
   B. $12x^2 + 7x + 10$
   C. $12x^2 + 7x-10$
   D. $12x^2-7x-10$

10. Perform the operation,
    $(-3x + 5xy-6y)-(4x + 2xy-5y)$.

    A. $-7x + 7xy-y$
    B. $-7x + 7xy-11y$
    C. $-7x + 3xy-y$
    D. $-7x + 3xy-11y$

11. Apply the polynomial identity to rewrite $x^2 + 20x + 100$.

    A. $x^2 + 100$
    B. $(x + 10)^2$
    C. $(x^2 + 10)^2$
    D. $(10x)^2$

12. Simplify $\frac{(-7)^2}{(-7)^{-1}}$.

    A. −343
    B. −49
    C. −21
    D. −7

13. The error on one manufacturing machine is 2×10^{-4}, and the error on a second machine is 8×10^{-5}. How many times larger is the error on the first machine?

    A. 1
    B. 2
    C. 3
    D. 4

14. Solve $x^2 = 225$.

    A. −5, 5
    B. −10, 10
    C. −15, 15
    D. −20, 20

15. In which of the following situations is probability sampling used?

    A. Qualitative research
    B. Studies with specific goals
    C. Randomly selected samples
    D. Studies with limited functions

16. A teacher wants to know if seat location affects test scores. What data needs to be collected for an experiment?

    A. The teacher should collect data on one seat for every class.
    B. The teacher should collect data on one student for every class.
    C. The teacher should collect data on a random sample of students for the final exam.
    D. The teacher should collect data on a random sample of students of test scores and seat location.

17. Identify the sampling technique that is a simple random sample for obtaining the opinion of grocery shoppers.

    A. Selecting 500 shoppers in the same city

    B. Selecting 500 shoppers who shop on Mondays

    C. Selecting 500 shoppers who bring in their children

    D. Selecting 500 shoppers by using a random number generator

18. If a letter is chosen at random from the word SUBSTITUTE, what is the probability that the letter chosen is "S" or "T"?

    A. $\frac{1}{5}$ C. $\frac{2}{5}$

    B. $\frac{3}{10}$ D. $\frac{1}{2}$

19. There are 60 students attending classes in town. There are 40 students in dance class and 30 students in art class. Find the number of students in either dance or art class.

    A. 30   C. 50

    B. 40   D. 60

20. Which option results in the greatest gain on an investment?

    A. 60% of gaining $5,000 and 40% of gaining $0

    B. 70% of gaining $4,500 and 30% of gaining $0

    C. 80% of gaining $4,000 and 20% of gaining $0

    D. 90% of gaining $3,500 and 10% of gaining $0

SECTION III. ADVANCED ALGEBRA AND FUNCTIONS

1. A half circle has an area of 45 square centimeters. Find the diameter to the nearest tenth of a centimeter. Use 3.14 for π.

   A. 2.7

   B. 5.4

   C. 10.8

   D. 16.2

2. The area of a half circle is 48 square centimeters. Find the circumference of the curved portion of the half circle to the nearest tenth of a centimeter. Use 3.14 for π.

   A. 17.3

   B. 24.5

   C. 34.5

   D. 49.0

3. Find the area in square millimeters of a circle with a radius of 9 millimeters. Round to the nearest hundredth. Use 3.14 for π.

   A. 56.52

   B. 254.34

   C. 508.68

   D. 1,017.36

4. What shape is used to measure the distance between two cities on a map?

   A. A ray

   B. A line

   C. A point

   D. A line segement

5. What is the number of symmetry lines for a regular hexagon?

   A. 2

   B. 4

   C. 6

   D. 8

6. Select the figure that is translated $(x - 4, y + 4)$.

A.

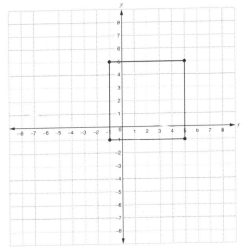

B.

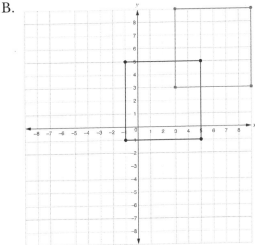

C.

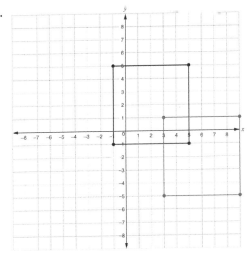

D.

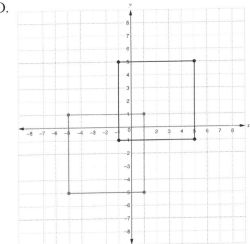

7. $\triangle GHI$ has points $G(2, 7)$, $H(-3, -8)$, and $I(-6, 0)$. After a transformation, the points are $G'(7, 2)$, $H'(-8, -3)$, and $I'(0, -6)$. What is the transformation between the points?

   A. Reflection across the x-axis

   B. Reflection across the y-axis

   C. Reflection across the line of $y = x$

   D. Reflection across the line of $y = -x$

8. If the multiple of some positive number is prime, which statement about that positive number is true?

   A. The positive number is prime.

   B. The positive number is equal to 0.

   C. The positive number is composite.

   D. None of the above.

9. Which number is a multiple of 123?

   A. −123   C. 247

   B. 1   D. 359

10. What is the minimum number of unique prime factors for a composite number?

   A. 0

   B. 1

   C. 2

   D. Not enough information

11. The base of an equilateral triangular pyramid has side lengths of 9 centimeters. The height of the triangular base is $3\sqrt{3}$ centimeters, and the pyramid has a height of 10 centimeters. Find the volume of the pyramid in cubic centimeters.

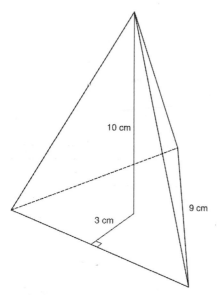

   A. $45\sqrt{3}$

   B. $90\sqrt{3}$

   C. $135\sqrt{3}$

   D. $180\sqrt{3}$

12. Find the height in centimeters of a cylinder with a volume of 800π cubic centimeters and a radius of 10 centimeters.

   A. 8

   B. 10

   C. 40

   D. 80

13. A paper cup in the shape of a cone has a diameter of 8 centimeters and a height of 11 centimeters. How much liquid does the cup hold if filled to the top? Use 3.14 for π.

   A. 92.11 cubic centimeters

   B. 184.21 cubic centimeters

   C. 368.42 cubic centimeters

   D. 736.84 cubic centimeters

14. A house is located at (15, 30). The next house is 100 meters away. What could be the coordinate of the second house?

   A. (15, 30)

   B. (30, 15)

   C. (115, 15)

   D. (115, 30)

15. Draw a square with the coordinates
    (−3, 4), (−3, −2), (3, −2), (3, 4).

A.

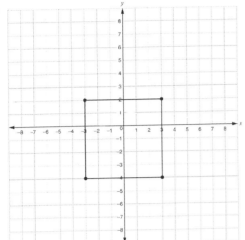

C.

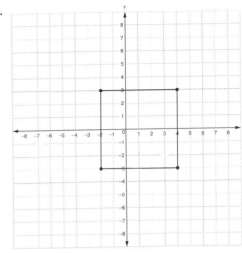

B.

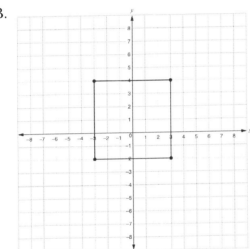

D.

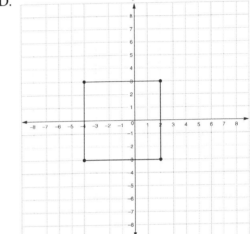

16. A cube has a side length of 15 millimeters. What is the volume in cubic millimeters?

    A. 45

    B. 1,350

    C. 3,375

    D. 6,750

17. A parallelogram has an area of 105 square inches. Find the height in inches if the base is 15 inches in length.

    A. 3

    B. 5

    C. 7

    D. 9

18. Solve the equation by completing the square, $x^2 - 2x - 37 = 0$.

    A. $-1 \pm \sqrt{37}$

    B. $1 \pm \sqrt{37}$

    C. $-1 \pm \sqrt{38}$

    D. $1 \pm \sqrt{38}$

19. Solve the equation by any method, $9x^2 - 48x + 64 = 0$.

    A. $-\frac{8}{3}$

    B. $-\frac{3}{8}$

    C. $\frac{3}{8}$

    D. $\frac{8}{3}$

20. Solve the equation by factoring, $6x^2 - 11x - 35 = 0$.

    A. $-\frac{5}{3}$ and $-\frac{7}{2}$

    B. $-\frac{5}{3}$ and $\frac{7}{2}$

    C. $\frac{5}{3}$ and $-\frac{7}{2}$

    D. $\frac{5}{3}$ and $\frac{7}{2}$

ACCUPLACER MATH PRACTICE EXAM 2
ANSWER KEY WITH EXPLANATORY ANSWERS

Section I. Arithmetic

1. C. The correct solution is adding two quantities with different units. To add quantities, they must have the same unit. For instance, adding a quantity of meters to a quantity of grams is impossible. **See Lesson: Basic Addition and Subtraction.**

2. C. The correct solution is 3,047. Place the digits in base-10 format, using the number of meters in the thousands place, the number of centimeters in the tens place, and the number of millimeters in the ones place. The measurement is 3,047 millimeters long. **See Lesson: Basic Addition and Subtraction.**

3. A. The correct solution is 1,078. Adding any number to 0 yields that number. On a number line, starting at a certain number and taking no steps in either direction yields the same number. **See Lesson: Basic Addition and Subtraction.**

4. A. The correct solution is 1,037. Use the subtraction algorithm. It will involve borrowing twice to get a number big enough to subtract in the ones place. **See Lesson: Basic Addition and Subtraction.**

5. B. Because 26 is not evenly divisible by 9, the best answer in this case has a remainder. The division algorithm is used to obtain this result. **See Lesson: Basic Multiplication and Division.**

6. C. Instead of adding the same number over and over (for example, $5 + 5 + 5 + 5 + 5 + 5$), multiplication enables a more concise expression. In this example, because the expression adds 6 terms of 5, it becomes 6×5, or 30. **See Lesson: Basic Multiplication and Division.**

7. C. When dividing signed numbers, remember that if the dividend and divisor have the same sign, the quotient is positive. Other than the sign, the process is the same as dividing whole numbers. **See Lesson: Basic Multiplication and Division.**

8. C. This question is asking for the remainder of division. The quotient of $203 \div 36$ is the number of class sections that are assigned a professor, and the remainder is the number of students left over. The remainder in this case is 23. Because 23 is not enough to fill a section, 23 students will not receive a slot. **See Lesson: Basic Multiplication and Division.**

9. C. The correct solution is 2.002 because 2.002 contains the smallest value in the tenths and the hundredths places. **See Lesson: Decimals and Fractions.**

10. A. The correct solution is $\frac{3}{8}$ because $\frac{0.375}{1} = \frac{375}{1000} = \frac{3}{8}$. **See Lesson: Decimals and Fractions.**

11. B. The correct answer is 20% because $\frac{1}{5}$ as a percent is $0.2 \times 100 = 20\%$. **See Lesson: Decimals and Fractions.**

12. A. The correct solution is the mean and median increase. The test score of 105 increases the mean from 85.67 to 87.6 and increases the median from 85 to 85.5. **See Lesson: Interpreting Categorical and Quantitative Data.**

13. C. The correct solution is the mean decreases, but the median does not change. The mean decreases from 46.75 to 44.83, but the median does not change from 46.5. **See Lesson: Interpreting Categorical and Quantitative Data.**

14. A. The correct solution is the median is greater for Company A, and the interquartile range is greater for Company A. The median is greater for Company A (50 hours versus 45 hours), and the interquartile range is greater for Company A (interquartile range is 30 hours versus 20 hours). **See Lesson: Interpreting Categorical and Quantitative Data.**

15. D. The correct solution is $1\frac{1}{2}$ because $\frac{3}{4} \times \frac{2}{1} = \frac{6}{4} = 1\frac{2}{4} = 1\frac{1}{2}$. **See Lesson: Multiplication and Division of Fractions.**

16. C. The correct solution is $\frac{8}{45}$ because $\frac{2}{3} \times \frac{4}{15} = \frac{8}{45}$. **See Lesson: Multiplication and Division of Fractions.**

17. D. The correct answer is $\frac{29}{35}$ because $\frac{29}{10} \div \frac{7}{2} = \frac{29}{10} \times \frac{2}{7} = \frac{58}{70} = \frac{29}{35}$. **See Lesson: Multiplication and Division of Fractions.**

18. D. The decimal 0.5 is equal to $\frac{1}{2}$, which is also equal to the ratio 1:2. But 1:2 odds are different because odds use colon notation in a different manner. **See Lesson: Ratios, Proportions, and Percentages.**

19. D. A number can take the form of an equivalent ratio, fraction, and percent. In contrast, a proportion is an equation rather than a pure number. **See Lesson: Ratios, Proportions, and Percentages.**

20. C. The company employs 273 men. If 35% of the company's employees are women, 65% are men. Set up a proportion using 65%, which is equal to $\frac{65}{100}$ or $\frac{13}{20}$:

$$\frac{13}{20} = \frac{?}{420}$$

The unknown number is the product of 13 and 420 ÷ 20 = 21, which is 273. **See Lesson: Ratios, Proportions, and Percentages.**

Section II. Quantitative Reasoning, Algebra, and Statistics

1. B. The correct solution is −10 because 10 is added to both sides of the equation. **See Lesson: Equations with One Variable.**

2. B. The correct solution is $x \geq -45$.

$10x-60 \leq 12x + 30$	Multiply all terms by the least common denominator of 15 to eliminate the fractions.
$-2x-60 \leq 30$	Subtract $12x$ from both sides of the inequality.
$-2x \leq 90$	Add 60 to both sides of the inequality.
$x \geq -45$	Divide both sides of the inequality by -2.

See Lesson: Equations with One Variable.

3. A. The correct solution is $\frac{2ab}{1-2a} = c$.

$2ab + 2ac = c$	Apply the distributive property.
$2ab = c-2ac$	Subtract $2ac$ from both sides of the equation.
$2ab = c(1-2a)$	Factor c from the right side of the equation.
$\frac{2ab}{1-2a} = c$	Divide both sides of the equation by $1-2a$.

See Lesson: Equations with One Variable.

4. D. The correct solution is $(9, 2)$.

$-4x + 12y = -12$	Multiply all terms in the first equation by 2.
$7y = 14$	Add the equations.
$y = 2$	Divide both sides of the equation by 7.
$-2x + 6(2) = -6$	Substitute 2 in the first equation for y.
$-2x + 12 = -6$	Simplify using order of operations.
$-2x = -18$	Subtract 12 from both sides of the equation.
$x = 9$	Divide both sides of the equation by -2.

See Lesson: Equations with Two Variables.

5. D. The correct graph has the two lines intersect at $(5, 2)$. **See Lesson: Equations with Two Variables.**

6. D. The correct solution is 147.5. The data set written in order is 120, 125, 130, 130, 145, 145, 150, 150, 150, 165, 170, 175. The middle two numbers are 145 and 150, and the mean of the numbers is 147.5. **See Lesson: Interpreting Graphics.**

7. C. The correct solution is 42, 44, and 45. The modes are 42, 44, and 45 because these values appear four times in the data set. **See Lesson: Interpreting Graphics.**

8. B. The correct solution is 15.25. The sum of all items is 183, and 183 and divided by 12 gives a mean of 15.25. **See Lesson: Interpreting Graphics.**

9. C. The correct solution is $12x^2 + 7x-10$.

$$(4x + 5)(3x-2) = 4x(3x-2) + 5(3x-2) = 12x^2-8x + 15x-10 = 12x^2 + 7x-10$$

See Lesson: Polynomials.

10. C. The correct solution is $-7x + 3xy-y$.

$$(-3x + 5xy-6y)-(4x + 2xy-5y) = (-3x + 5xy-6y) + (-4x-2xy + 5y)$$
$$= (-3x-4x) + (5xy-2xy) + (-6y + 5y) = -7x + 3xy-y$$

See Lesson: Polynomials.

11. B. The correct solution is $(x + 10)^2$. The expression $x^2 + 20x + 100$ is rewritten as $(x + 10)^2$ because the value of a is x and the value of b is 10. **See Lesson: Polynomials.**

12. A. The correct solution is -343 because $\frac{(-7)^2}{(-7)^{-1}} = (-7)^{2-(-1)} = (-7)^3 = -343$. **See Lesson: Powers, Exponents, Roots, and Radicals.**

13. C. The correct solution is 3 because 2×10^{-4} is 0.0002 and 8×10^{-5} is 0.00008. So, the error on the first machine is about 3 times larger. **See Lesson: Powers, Exponents, Roots, and Radicals.**

14. C. The correct solution is -15, 15 because the square root of 225 is 15. The values of -15 and 15 make the equation true. **See Lesson: Powers, Exponents, Roots, and Radicals.**

15. C. The correct solution is randomly selected samples because random sampling techniques are used. **See Lesson: Statistical Measures.**

16. D. The correct solution is that the teacher should collect data on a random sample of students of test scores and seat location because there are specific groups based on seat location. **See Lesson: Statistical Measures.**

17. D. The correct solution is selecting 500 shoppers by using a random number generator because each shopper has the same chance of being selected. **See Lesson: Statistical Measures.**

18. D. The correct solution is $\frac{1}{2}$. There are 3 S's and 2 T's in the word SUBTITUTE out of 10 letters. The probability is $\frac{3}{10} + \frac{2}{10} = \frac{5}{10} = \frac{1}{2}$. **See Lesson: Statistics & Probability: The Rules of Probability.**

19. C. The correct solution 50 because there are 70 students in both classes less the total students is 10 students. Then, subtract 10 students from the total, which is 50 students. **See Lesson: Statistics & Probability: The Rules of Probability.**

20. C. The correct solution is 80% of gaining \$4,000 and 20% of gaining \$0. The expected value is $0.80(40) = \$3,200$. **See Lesson: Statistics & Probability: The Rules of Probability.**

Section III. Advanced Algebra and Functions

1. C. The correct solution is 10.8 because $A = \frac{1}{2}\pi r^2; 45 = \left(\frac{1}{2}\right)3.14 r^2; 45 = 1.57 r^2 = 28.66 = r^2, r \approx 5.4$. The diameter is twice the radius, or about 10.8 centimeters. **See Lesson: Circles.**

2. A. The correct solution is 17.3. $A = \frac{1}{2}\pi r^2; 48 = \frac{1}{2}(3.14) r^2; 48 = 1.57 r^2; 30.57 = r^2; r \approx 5.5$ centimeters. $C = \frac{1}{2}(2\pi r); C = \frac{1}{2}(2)(3.14)(5.5) \approx 17.3$ centimeters. **See Lesson: Circles.**

3. B. The correct solution is 254.34 because $A = \pi r^2 \approx 3.14(9)^2 \approx 3.14(81) \approx 254.34$ square millimeters. **See Lesson: Circles.**

4. D. The correct solution is line segment because the cities represent the endpoints and the segment is the distance between the two points. **See Lesson: Congruence.**

5. C. The correct solution is six lines of symmetry. There are three lines of symmetry through opposite vertices and three lines through the midpoints of opposite segments. **See Lesson: Congruence.**

6. D. The correct solution is D. The translation for the points is $(x - 4, y + 4)$. The points of the original square, (–1, 5), (–1, –1), (5, –1) and (5, 5), become (–5, 9), (–5, 3), (1, 3) and (1, 9). **See Lesson: Congruence.**

7. C. The correct solution is a reflection across the line of $y = x$ because the points (x, y) become (y, x). **See Lesson: Congruence.**

8. D. If the positive number is 1, then one of its multiples is 3—a prime number. Answer A is therefore false, as is answer C. If the positive number is 0, all of its multiples are 0. Therefore, it has no prime multiples, eliminating answer B. **See Lesson: Factors and Multiples.**

9. A. Any product of a number and an integer is a multiple of that number. Since 123 × –1 is –123, one multiple of 123 is –123. **See Lesson: Factors and Multiples.**

10. B. A prime number has only 1 and itself as factors; therefore, a composite number must have at least one other factor. If that factor is composite, the number has more factors. If that factor is prime, then it is the only prime factor of the number. For example, 9 has 3 as a prime factor; its only other factors are 1 and 9. But 1 is not a prime number. Neither is 9, which is composite. A composite number therefore has at least one unique prime factor. **See Lesson: Factors and Multiples.**

11. A. The correct solution is $45\sqrt{3}$. Substitute the values into the formula and simplify using the order of operations, $V = \frac{1}{3}Bh = \frac{1}{3}\left(\frac{1}{2}bh\right)h = \frac{1}{3}\left(\frac{1}{2}(9)(3\sqrt{3})\right)10 = 45\sqrt{3}$ cubic centimeters. **See Lesson: Measurement and Dimension.**

12. A. The correct solution is 8. Substitute the values into the formula, $800\pi = \pi 10^2 h$, and apply the exponent, $800\pi = \pi(100)h$. Then, divide both sides of the equation by 100π, $h = 8$ centimeters. **See Lesson: Measurement and Dimension.**

13. B. The correct solution is 184.21 cubic centimeters. The radius is 4 centimeters. Substitute the values into the formula and simplify using the order of operations, $V = \frac{1}{3}\pi r^2 h = \frac{1}{3}(3.14)4^2(11) = \frac{1}{3}(3.14)(16)(11) = 184.21$ cubic centimeters. **See Lesson: Measurement and Dimension.**

14. D. The correct solution is (115, 30) because 100 can be added to the x-coordinate, $15 + 100 = 115$. **See Lesson: Similarity, Right Triangles, and Trigonometry.**

15. B. The first point is in the second quadrant, the second point is in the third quadrant, the third point is in the fourth quadrant, and the last point is in the first quadrant. **See Lesson: Similarity, Right Triangles, and Trigonometry.**

16. C. The correct solution is 3,375. Substitute the values into the formula and simplify using the order of operations, $V = s^3 = 15^3 = 3,375$ cubic millimeters. **See Lesson: Similarity, Right Triangles, and Trigonometry.**

17. C. The correct solution is 7. Substitute the values into the formula, $105 = 15h$ and divide both sides of the equation by 15, $h = 7$ inches. **See Lesson: Similarity, Right Triangles, and Trigonometry.**

18. D. The correct solutions are $1 \pm \sqrt{38}$.

$x^2 - 2x = 37$	Add 37 to both sides of the equation.
$x^2 - 2x + 1 = 37 + 1$	Complete the square, $\left(\frac{2}{2}\right)^2 = 1^2 = 1$.

Add 1 to both sides of the equation.

$x^2 - 2x + 1 = 38$	Simplify the right side of the equation.
$(x-1)^2 = 38$	Factor the left side of the equation.
$x - 1 = \pm\sqrt{38}$	Apply the square root to both sides of the equation.
$x = 1 \pm \sqrt{38}$	Add 1 to both sides of the equation.

See Lesson: Solving Quadratic Equations.

19. D. The correct solution is $\frac{8}{3}$. The equation can be solved by factoring.

$(3x-8)(3x-8) = 0$	Factor the equation.
$(3x-8) = 0\ (3x-8) = 0$	Set each factor equal to 0.
$(3x-8) = 0$	Set one factor equal to zero because both factors are the same.
$3x - 8 = 0$	Add 8 to both sides of the equation and divide both sides of the equation by 3 to solve.
$3x = 8$	
$x = \frac{8}{3}$	

See Lesson: Solving Quadratic Equations.

20. B. The correct solutions are $-\frac{5}{3}$ and $\frac{7}{2}$.

$(3x + 5)(2x–7) = 0$	Factor the equation.
$(3x + 5) = 0$ or $(2x–7) = 0$	Set each factor equal to 0.
$3x + 5 = 0$	Subtract 5 from both sides of the equation and divide both sides of the equation by 3 to solve.
$3x = –5$	
$x = -\frac{5}{3}$	
$2x–7 = 0$	Add 7 to both sides of the equation and divide both sides of the equation by 2 to solve.
$2x = 7$	
$x = \frac{7}{2}$	

See Lesson: Solving Quadratic Equations.

Accuplacer Math Practice Exam 3

Section I. Arithmetic

1. How much change should a customer expect if she is buying a $53 item and hands the cashier two $50 bills?

    A. $3

    B. $47

    C. $57

    D. $100

2. Which mathematical statement is true?

    A. $-3 = 3$

    B. $3 < -3$

    C. $3 > -3$

    D. None of the above.

3. What is $4 + 5 + 12 + 9$?

    A. 20

    B. 30

    C. 40

    D. 50

4. What is $743 - 744$?

    A. -1

    B. 0

    C. 1

    D. 1,487

5. Evaluate the expression $(3 \times (4 + 9) \div 13 - 2) + 1.$

    A. -2

    B. 0

    C. 2

    D. 5

6. Which expression yields a quotient with no remainder?

    A. $5 \div 5$

    B. $26 \div 5$

    C. $81 \div 40$

    D. $365 \div 87$

7. When dealing with a series of multiplication and division operations, which is the correct approach to evaluating them?

    A. Evaluate all division operations first.

    B. Evaluate the expression from left to right.

    C. Evaluate all multiplication operations first.

    D. None of the above.

8. Evaluate the expression $3 + 1 - 5 + 2 - 6.$

    A. -9

    B. -5

    C. 0

    D. 17

9. Which fraction is the greatest?

    A. $\frac{5}{12}$

    B. $\frac{1}{3}$

    C. $\frac{1}{6}$

    D. $\frac{1}{4}$

10. Write 29% as a decimal.

    A. 29

    B. 2.9

    C. 0.29

    D. 0.029

11. Write $1\frac{11}{20}$ as a percent.

    A. 150%

    B. 155%

    C. 200%

    D. 205%

12. The wait times in minutes for the last 15 customers at a restaurant are 20, 17, 18, 15, 19, 45, 22, 18, 25, 28, 16, 19, 23, 20, 25. What is the effect of removing the outlier on the mean and median?

    A. The mean and median decrease.

    B. There is no change to the mean or median.

    C. The mean decreases, but there is no change to the median.

    D. The median decreases, but there is no change to the mean.

13. The list shows the commute time of workers on two different streets.

    Street 1: 5, 5, 10, 10, 10, 15, 15, 15, 15, 15, 15, 20, 20, 20, 25, 25, 30, 30, 35, 40, 45

    Street 2: 5, 10, 15, 15, 20, 20, 20, 20, 25, 25, 25, 30, 30, 30, 30, 30, 30, 35, 40, 45, 45

    Which statement describes the median and interquartile range?

    A. Street 1 had the greater median, but Street 2 had a higher interquartile range.

    B. Street 2 had the greater median, but Street 1 had a higher interquartile range.

    C. Street 1 had the greater median, and Street 1 had a higher interquartile range.

    D. Street 2 had the greater median, and Street 2 had a higher interquartile range.

14. Identify the variable from a census study that is categorical.

    A. Age

    B. Zip code

    C. Family size

    D. Annual income

15. Multiply $2 \times \frac{3}{4}$.

    A. $\frac{1}{4}$

    B. $\frac{3}{8}$

    C. $1\frac{1}{2}$

    D. $2\frac{3}{4}$

16. Divide $3\frac{1}{2} \div 2\frac{1}{2}$.

    A. $1\frac{1}{4}$

    B. $1\frac{2}{5}$

    C. $1\frac{1}{2}$

    D. $1\frac{2}{3}$

17. Multiply $1\frac{1}{2} \times 2\frac{1}{3}$.

    A. $3\frac{1}{6}$

    B. $3\frac{1}{5}$

    C. $3\frac{1}{4}$

    D. $3\frac{1}{2}$

18. If a company's automobile fleet includes 132 cars of brand A and 48 cars of brand B, what is the fleet's ratio of brand B to brand A?

    A. 4:11

    B. 11:15

    C. 15:11

    D. 11:4

19. If a truck's initial speed is 60 mph and its final speed is 100 mph, what is its percent change in speed?

    A. 17%

    B. 33%

    C. 40%

    D. 67%

20. What is 36% as a ratio?

    A. 9:25

    B. 36:100

    C. 18:40

    D. 25:9

SECTION II. QUANTITATIVE REASONING, ALGEBRA, AND STATISTICS

1. Solve the inequality for the unknown,
   $3(4x–1) > 5(2x + 3)$.

   A. $x > 2$ C. $x > 10$

   B. $x > 9$ D. $x > 18$

2. Solve the equation for the unknown,
   $\frac{1}{2}x + 3 = \frac{1}{4}x–2$.

   A. $–20$ C. 10

   B. $–10$ D. 20

3. Solve the equation for the unknown,
   $2(x–4) = 5(x + 2)$.

   A. $–24$ C. $–6$

   B. $–12$ D. $–2$

4. Solve the system of equations,
   $$x + 2y = 5$$
   $$-5x + 3y = -25$$

   A. $(5, 0)$ C. $(-5, 0)$

   B. $(0, -5)$ D. $(0, 5)$

5. Solve the system of equations by graphing,
   $$6x + 5y = -7$$
   $$2x–4y = -8$$

   A.

   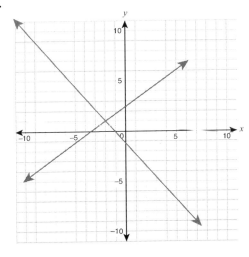

B.

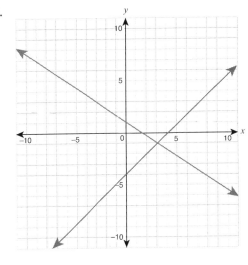

C.

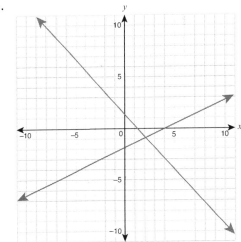

D.

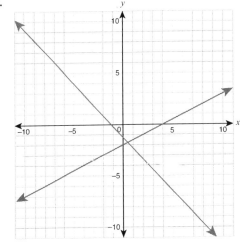

6. The bar chart shows the number of boys and girls who participate in sports. What year had the most participants?

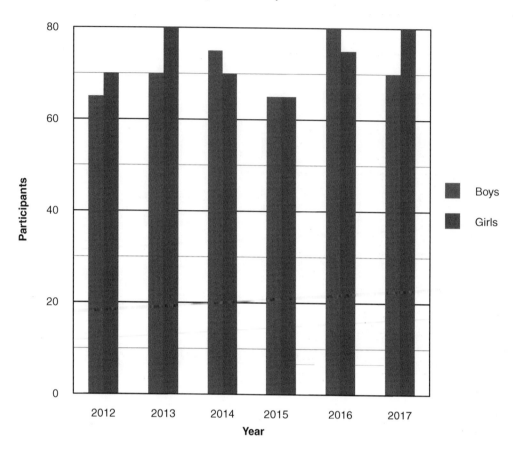

A. 2013

C. 2016

B. 2014

D. 2017

7. Find the median for the data set 20, 22, 23, 24, 25, 21, 20, 22, 24, 25, 23, 22, 25, 26, 22, and 20.

A. 22

C. 22.5

B. 22.25

D. 22.75

8. The double line chart shows the number of points scored and points given up by a basketball team over the first 10 games. Which statement is true?

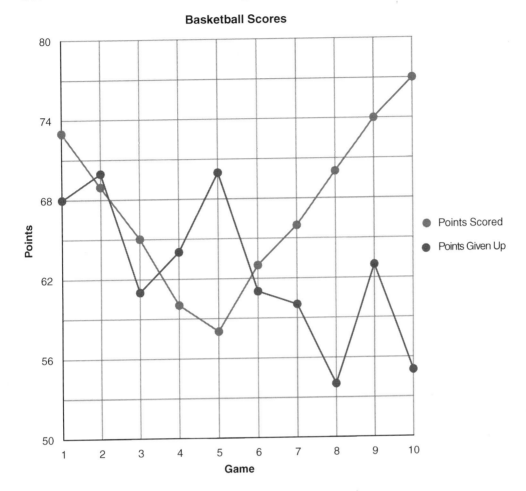

Basketball Scores

A. The team scored more than 62 points in a majority of games and gave up fewer than 62 points in a majority of games.

B. The team scored more than 65 points in a majority of games and gave up fewer than 65 points in a majority of games.

C. The team scored more than 68 points in a majority of games and gave up fewer than 68 points in a majority of games.

D. The team scored more than 70 points in a majority of games and gave up fewer than 65 points in a majority of games.

9. Multiply, $(2y^2-1)(y^2-3y+5)$.

A. $2y^4-6y^3+10y^2+3y-5$

B. $2y^4-6y^3+9y^2+3y-5$

C. $2y^4-6y^3+11y^2+3y-5$

D. $2y^4-6y^3+8y^2+3y-5$

10. Perform the operation, $(4y^3+5y^2-6y)+(7y^2+2y-5)$.

A. $4y^3+12y^2+4y-5$

B. $4y^3+10y^2-4y-5$

C. $4y^3+12y^2-4y-5$

D. $4y^3+10y^2+4y-5$

11. Apply the polynomial identity to rewrite x^2-100.

   A. $(x-10)^2$

   B. $(x-10)(x+10)$

   C. $(x+10)^2$

   D. x^2-10^2

12. Simplify $\left(\frac{x^0}{y^{-2}}\right)^2$.

   A. $\frac{1}{y^4}$

   B. $\frac{x}{y^4}$

   C. y^4

   D. $x^4 y^4$

13. The error in connecting two pipes for one house is 3×10^{-5} meter, and the error in connecting two pipes for a second house is about 1×10^{-6} meter. How many times larger is the error in the first house?

   A. 3

   B. 30

   C. 300

   D. 3,000

14. Solve $x^2 = 81$.

   A. $-6, 6$

   B. $-7, 7$

   C. $-8, 8$

   D. $-9, 9$

15. There are four available pen colors to choose. A simulation is used to represent the number of times each pen is used.

Red	Blue	Black	Green	Total
1,248	1,260	1,247	1,245	5,000

Choose the statement that correctly explains why or why not seeing these results questions the probability of one out of four for each color.

   A. Yes, because of the limited number of outcomes

   B. Yes, because not enough simulations were completed

   C. No, because the probability of each color is not exactly one out of four

   D. No, because the probability of each color is very close to one out of four

16. Identify the study that is a census.

   A. A restaurant asks all customers what they want to add to the menu.

   B. A restaurant asks some of its customers what they want to add to the menu.

   C. A restaurant asks all customers on a Friday what they want to add to the menu.

   D. A restaurant asks random customers by email what they want to add to the menu.

17. A survey group wants to ask the daily commute time for workers at a large company who use a car to get to work. What is the sample for the survey?

   A. Employees who work from home

   B. Employees who drive to work daily

   C. Employees who work for the company

   D. Employees who drive on a highway to work daily

18. A spinner contains numbers 1–20. What is the probability of spinning a multiple of 3 or a multiple of 5?

   A. $\frac{3}{10}$

   B. $\frac{1}{5}$

   C. $\frac{9}{20}$

   D. $\frac{11}{20}$

19. A club wants to meet once a week. The available times are Tuesday, Wednesday, and Thursday at 2:00 p.m., 3:00 p.m., and 4:00 p.m. How many outcomes are there for the sample space?

   A. 3

   B. 6

   C. 9

   D. 12

20. Alex and Amir play soccer, Muhammad and David play tennis, and Ji-ho and Frank play both. Describe a union of the people who play soccer or tennis.

A. Muhammad and David

B. Ji-ho and Frank

C. Alex, Amir, Ji-ho, and Frank

D. Alex, Amir, Muhammad, David, Ji-ho, and Frank

SECTION III. ADVANCED ALGEBRA AND FUNCTIONS

1. A circle has an area of 12 square feet. Find the diameter to the nearest tenth of a foot. Use 3.14 for π.

   A. 1.0   C. 3.0

   B. 2.0   D. 4.0

2. The circumference of a circle is 92 centimeters. Find the area of the circle to the nearest tenth of a square centimeter. Use 3.14 for π.

   A. 669.3   C. 1,338.6

   B. 858.5   D. 2,695.7

3. Find the circumference in centimeters of a circle with a radius of 11 centimeters. Use 3.14 for π.

   A. 3.14   C. 34.54

   B. 6.28   D. 69.08

4. What is the number of symmetry lines for an isosceles trapezoid?

   A. 0   C. 2

   B. 1   D. 3

5. Select the statement that is true for the angles.

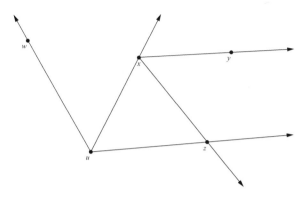

   A. Points X and Y are vertices of angles.

   B. Points X and U are vertices of angles.

   C. Points W and Y are vertices of angles.

   D. Points W and U are vertices of angles.

6. $\triangle MNO$ has points $M(2, 6)$, $N(3, -1)$, and $O(0, -2)$. After a transformation, the points are $M'(-1, 2)$, $N'(0, -5)$, and $O'(-3, -6)$. What is the transformation between the points?

   A. Translation right 3 units and up 4 units

   B. Translation left 3 units and up 4 units

   C. Translation right 3 units and down 4 units

   D. Translation left 3 units and down 4 units

7. Select the figure that is rotated 90° counterclockwise about the origin.

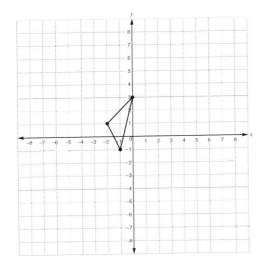

A.

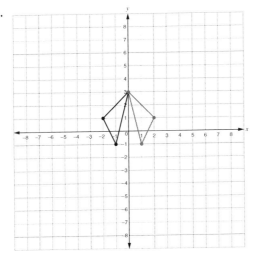

B.

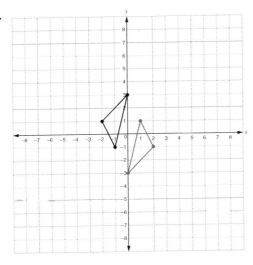

C.

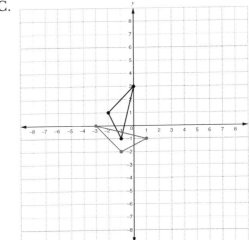

D.

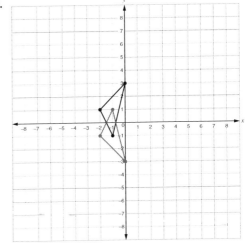

8. What are the prime factors of 30?

   A. 5, 6

   B. 2, 3, 5

   C. 1, 3, 10

   D. 2, 3, 5, 6, 10, 15

9. If x is divisible by y, which statement best relates x and y?

   A. y is a factor of x.

   B. x is a multiple of y.

   C. x and y are whole numbers.

   D. All of the above.

10. Which statement best describes the branches of a factor tree in a prime factorization?

    A. Prime factors

    B. Odd numbers

    C. Even numbers

    D. Composite factors

11. A basketball has a diameter of 10 inches. What is the volume in cubic inches inside the ball? Use 3.14 for π.

    A. 261.67

    B. 523.33

    C. 1,046.67

    D. 2,093.33

12. The volume of a hemi-sphere is $\frac{16}{3}\pi$ cubic feet. What is the diameter in feet?

    A. 1

    B. 2

    C. 3

    D. 4

13. The volume of a cone is 28π cubic inches, and its diameter is 2 inches. What is the height of the cone?

    A. 2 inches

    B. 4 inches

    C. 6 inches

    D. 8 inches

14. An outdoor game board is 20 feet by 30 feet. One corner of the game board on the coordinate plane is $(-10, -20)$. What could be a second coordinate of the game board?

    A. $(-20, -10)$

    B. $(-10, 10)$

    C. $(10, -10)$

    D. $(-20, 10)$

15. A right triangular prism has a base area of 63 square inches and a height of 10 inches. What is the volume in cubic inches?

    A. 63

    B. 126

    C. 315

    D. 630

16. Given the coordinates for a square $(-6, 6)$, $(6, 6)$, $(6, -6)$, $(-6, -6)$, find the length of each side of the square.

    A. 0 units

    B. 6 units

    C. 12 units

    D. 18 units

17 Draw a triangle with the coordinates $(-5,0), (-1,0), (5,3)$.

A.
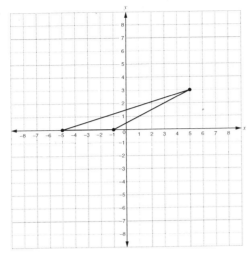

C.
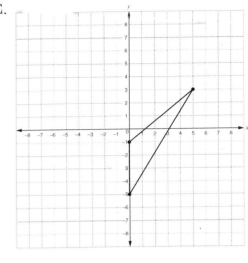

B.
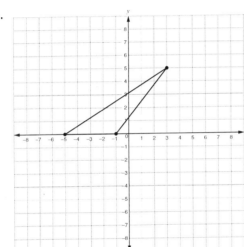

D.
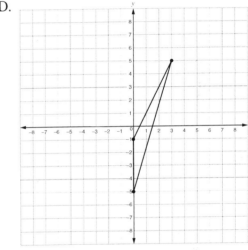

18. Solve the equation by any method, $x^2 + 17x + 20 = 0$.

A. −15.73 and −1.27

B. 15.73 and −1.27

C. −15.73 and 1.27

D. 15.73 and 1.27

19. Solve the equation by the square root method, $4x^2 - 10 = 15$.

A. $\pm \frac{5}{4}$

B. $\pm \frac{5}{2}$

C. $\pm \frac{25}{4}$

D. $\pm \frac{25}{2}$

20. Solve the equation by factoring, $x^2 - 13x + 30 = 0$.

A. −3, −10

B. −3, 10

C. 3, −10

D. 3, 10

ACCUPLACER MATH PRACTICE EXAM 3
ANSWER KEY WITH EXPLANATORY ANSWERS

Section I. Arithmetic

1. B. The correct solution is $47. The customer gives the cashier $100, which is the sum of $50 and $50. To find out how much change she receives, calculate the difference between $100 and $53, which is $47. **See Lesson: Basic Addition and Subtraction.**

2. C. The correct solution is $3 > -3$. A negative number is always less than a positive number. Try placing 3 and -3 on the number line to show that $3 > -3$. **See Lesson: Basic Addition and Subtraction.**

3. B. The correct solution is 30. Use the addition algorithm or a number line. Mental addition is also an option because the numbers are small. **See Lesson: Basic Addition and Subtraction.**

4. A. The correct solution is -1. This subtraction is easy to see on a number line or by inspection because the numbers are close. Remember that when subtracting a larger number from a smaller one, the difference is negative. **See Lesson: Basic Addition and Subtraction.**

5. C. Follow the order of operations (the PEMDAS mnemonic). Begin with the innermost parentheses and work outward, multiplying and dividing from left to right before adding and subtracting from left to right. **See Lesson: Basic Multiplication and Division.**

$(3 \times (4 + 9) \div 13 - 2) + 1$

$(3 \times 13 \div 13 - 2) + 1$

$(39 \div 13 - 2) + 1$

$(3 - 2) + 1$

$1 + 1$

2

6. A. By inspection, $5 \div 5 = 1$, so it has no remainder. Using the division algorithm on the other expressions produces a remainder. **See Lesson: Basic Multiplication and Division.**

7. B. Multiplication and division have equivalent priority in the order of operations. In this case, the expression must be evaluated from left to right. **See Lesson: Basic Multiplication and Division.**

8. B. This expression only involves addition and subtraction, but its evaluation must go from left to right. **See Lesson: Basic Multiplication and Division.**

$$3 + 1 - 5 + 2 - 6$$
$$4 - 5 + 2 - 6$$
$$(-1) + 2 - 6$$
$$1 - 6$$
$$-5$$

9. A. The correct solution is $\frac{5}{12}$ because $\frac{5}{12}$ has the largest numerator when comparing to the other fractions with the same denominator. The fractions with a common denominator of 12 are $\frac{5}{12} = \frac{5}{12}, \frac{1}{3} = \frac{4}{12}, \frac{1}{6} = \frac{2}{12}, \frac{1}{4} = \frac{3}{12}$. **See Lesson: Decimals and Fractions.**

10. C. The correct answer is 0.29 because 29% as a decimal is $29 \div 100 = 0.29$. **See Lesson: Decimals and Fractions.**

11. B. The correct answer is 155% because $1\frac{11}{20}$ as a percent is $1.55 \times 100 = 155\%$. **See Lesson: Decimals and Fractions.**

12. A. The correct solution is mean and median decrease. The mean time decreases from 22 to 20.36 minutes, and the median time decreases from 20 minutes to 19.5 minutes. **See Lesson: Interpreting Categorical and Quantitative Data.**

13. D. The correct solution is Street 2 had the greater median, and Street 2 had a higher interquartile range. The larger median is Street 2. The higher interquartile range is Street 2, which means the data is more spread out from the median. **See Lesson: Interpreting Categorical and Quantitative Data.**

14. B. The correct solution is zip code because it classifies based on location and is a number that does not make sense to average. **See Lesson: Interpreting Categorical and Quantitative Data.**

15. C. The correct solution is $1\frac{1}{2}$ because $\frac{2}{1} \times \frac{3}{4} = \frac{6}{4} = 1\frac{2}{4} = 1\frac{1}{2}$. **See Lesson: Multiplication and Division of Fractions.**

16. B. The correct answer is $1\frac{2}{5}$ because $\frac{7}{2} \div \frac{5}{2} = \frac{7}{2} \times \frac{2}{5} = \frac{14}{10} = 1\frac{4}{10} = 1\frac{2}{5}$. **See Lesson: Multiplication and Division of Fractions.**

17. D. The correct solution is $3\frac{1}{2}$ because $\frac{3}{2} \times \frac{7}{3} = \frac{21}{6} = 3\frac{3}{6} = 3\frac{1}{2}$. **See Lesson: Multiplication and Division of Fractions.**

18. A. The ratio is 4:11. A ratio is like a fraction of two numbers, although in this case the answer uses colon notation. The ratio of brand B to brand A is the number of brand-B cars divided by the number of brand-A cars. Reduce to lowest terms:

$$\frac{48}{132} = \frac{4}{11}$$

See Lesson: Ratios, Proportions, and Percentages.

19. D. The truck has a 67% change in speed. The truck's change in speed is the difference between its final and initial speed: in this case, 100 mph – 60 mph = 40 mph. To find the percent change, divide 40 mph by the initial speed (60 mph) and then multiply by 100%.

$$\frac{40 \text{ mph}}{60 \text{ mph}} \times 100\% = 0.67 \times 100\% = 67\%$$

See Lesson: Ratios, Proportions, and Percentages.

20. A. As a ratio, 36% is 9:25. The most direct route is to convert 36% to a fraction, $\frac{36}{100}$, then reduce to lowest terms: $\frac{9}{25}$. The equivalent ratio in colon notation is 9:25. **See Lesson: Ratios, Proportions, and Percentages.**

Section II. Quantitative Reasoning, Algebra, and Statistics

1. B. The correct solution is $x > 9$.

$12x{-}3 > 10x + 15$	Apply the distributive property.
$2x{-}3 > 15$	Subtract $10x$ from both sides of the inequality.
$2x > 18$	Add 3 to both sides of the inequality.
$x > 9$	Divide both sides of the inequality by 2.

See Lesson: Equations with One Variable.

2. A. The correct solution is –20.

$2x + 12 = x{-}8$	Multiply all terms by the least common denominator of 4 to eliminate the fractions.
$x + 12 = -8$	Subtract x from both sides of the equation.
$x = -20$	Subtract 12 from both sides of the equation.

See Lesson: Equations with One Variable.

3. C. The correct solution is –6.

$2x{-}8 = 5x + 10$	Apply the distributive property.
$-3x{-}8 = 10$	Subtract $5x$ from both sides of the equation.
$-3x = 18$	Add 8 to both sides of the equation.
$x = -6$	Divide both sides of the equation by –3.

See Lesson: Equations with One Variable.

4. A. The correct solution is (5, 0).

$x = -2y + 5$	Solve the first equation for x by subtracting $2y$ from both sides of the equation.
$-5(-2y + 5) + 3y = -25$	Substitute $-2y + 5$ in for x in the first equation.
$10y{-}25 + 3y = -25$	Apply the distributive property.
$13y{-}25 = -25$	Combine like terms on the left side of the equation.
$13y = 0$	Add 25 to both sides of the equation.
$y = 0$	Divide both sides of the equation by 13.
$x + 2(0) = 5$	Substitute 0 in the second equation for y.
$x = 5$	Simplify using order of operations.

See Lesson: Equations with Two Variables.

5. C. The correct graph has the two lines intersect at (-2, 1). **See Lesson: Equations with Two Variables.**

6. C. The correct solution is 2016 because there were 155 total participants. **See Lesson: Interpreting Graphics.**

7. C. The correct solution is 22.5. The data set written in order is 20, 20, 20, 21, 22, 22, 22, 22, 23, 23, 24, 24, 25, 25, 25 and 26. The middle two numbers are 22 and 23, and the mean of these numbers is 22.5. **See Lesson: Interpreting Graphics.**

8. B. The correct solution is the team scored more than 65 points in a majority of games and gave up fewer than 65 points in a majority of games. From the graph, there are 6 games during which the team scored more than 65 points and 6 games during which it gave up fewer than 65 points. **See Lesson: Interpreting Graphics.**

9. B. The correct solution is $2y^4{-}6y^3 + 9y^2 + 3y{-}5$.

$$(2y^2{-}1)(y^2{-}3y + 5) = (2y^2{-}1)(y^2) + (2y^2{-}1)(-3y) + (2y^2{-}1)(5)$$
$$= 2y^4{-}y^2{-}6y^3 + 3y + 10y^2{-}5 = 2y^4{-}6y^3 + 9y^2 + 3y{-}5$$

See Lesson: Polynomials.

10. C. The correct solution is $4y^3 + 12y^2{-}4y{-}5$.

$$(4y^3 + 5y^2{-}6y) + (7y^2 + 2y{-}5) = 4y^3 + (5y^2 + 7y^2) + (-6y + 2y){-}5 = 4y^3 + 12y^2{-}4y{-}5$$

See Lesson: Polynomials.

11. B. The correct solution is $(x{-}10)(x + 10)$. The expression $x^2{-}100$ is rewritten as $(x{-}10)(x + 10)$ because the value of a is x and the value of b is 10. **See Lesson: Polynomials.**

12. C. The correct solution is y^4 because $\left(\frac{x^0}{y^{-2}}\right)^2 = \frac{x^{0\times2}}{y^{-2\times2}} = \frac{x^0}{y^{-4}} = \frac{1}{y^{-4}} = y^4$. **See Lesson: Powers, Exponents, Roots, and Radicals.**

13. B. The correct solution is 30 because 3×10^{-5} is 0.00003 and 1×10^{-6} is 0.000001. So, the first error is 30 times larger. **See Lesson: Powers, Exponents, Roots, and Radicals.**

14. D. The correct solution is –9, 9 because the square root of 81 is 9. The values of –9 and 9 make the equation true. **See Lesson: Powers, Exponents, Roots, and Radicals.**

15. D. The correct solution is no, because the probability of each color is very close to one out of four. The more simulations, the closer the results will be to the actual probability of one out of four for each color. **See Lesson: Statistical Measures.**

16. A. The correct solution is a restaurant asking all customers what they want to add to the menu because all customers are being asked their opinion. **See Lesson: Statistical Measures.**

17. B. The correct solution is employees who drive to work daily because this sample represents an accurate sample from the population of all employees. **See Lesson: Statistical Measures.**

18. C. The correct solution is $\frac{9}{20}$. There are six multiples of 3 and four multiples of 5. The overlap of 15 is subtracted from the probability, $\frac{6}{20} + \frac{4}{20} - \frac{1}{20} = \frac{9}{20}$. **See Lesson: Statistics & Probability: The Rules of Probability.**

19. C. The correct solution is 9 possible outcomes. There are three days and three times available, or 3 times 3, which is 9 times. **See Lesson: Statistics & Probability: The Rules of Probability.**

20. D. The correct solution is Alex, Amir, Muhammad, David, Ji-ho, and Frank because the union describes all people playing soccer or tennis. **See Lesson: Statistics & Probability: The Rules of Probability.**

Section III. Advanced Algebra and Functions

1. D. The correct solution is 4.0 because $A = \pi r^2$; $12 = 3.14 r^2$; $3.82 = r^2$; $r \approx 2.0$. The diameter is twice the radius, or about 4.0 feet. **See Lesson: Circles.**

2. A. The correct solution is 669.3. $C = 2\pi r$; $92 = 2(3.14)r$; $92 = 6.28r$; $r \approx 14.6$ centimeters. $A = \pi r^2 \approx 3.14(14.6)^2 \approx 3.14(213.16) \approx 669.3$ square centimeters. **See Lesson: Circles.**

3. D. The correct solution is 69.08 because $C = 2\pi r \approx (2)3.14(11) \approx 69.08$ centimeters. **See Lesson: Circles.**

4. B. The correct solution is one line of symmetry. There is a vertical line of symmetry that maps the isosceles trapezoid onto itself. **See Lesson: Congruence.**

5. B. The correct solution is points X and U are vertices of angles because these points are the intersection of two rays. **See Lesson: Congruence.**

6. D. The correct solution is a translation left 3 units and down 4 units because the points (x, y) become $(x - 3, y - 4)$. **See Lesson: Congruence.**

7. C. The correct solution is C. This is a rotation of $90°$ counterclockwise because the point (x, y) becomes $(-y, x)$. **See Lesson: Congruence.**

8. B. Answers A, C, and D all contain composite numbers (6, 10, and 15). Therefore, answer B is correct. **See Lesson: Factors and Multiples.**

9. D. Each statement about x and y is true. By definition, if one number is a factor of another, both are whole numbers. **See Lesson: Factors and Multiples.**

10. D. The leaves of a factor tree in a prime factorization are prime factors. But the branches, because they are not leaves, are composite—yet they are still factors of the number undergoing prime factorization. Branches may be even or odd because some composite numbers are even and some are odd. **See Lesson: Factors and Multiples.**

11. B. The correct solution is 523.33 cubic inches. The radius is 5 inches. Substitute the values into the formula and simplify using the order of operations, $V = \frac{4}{3}\pi r^3 = \frac{4}{3}(3.14)5^3 = \frac{4}{3}(3.14)(125) = 523.33$ cubic inches. **See Lesson: Measurement and Dimension.**

12. D. The correct solution is 4 feet. Substitute the values into the formula $\frac{16}{3}\pi = \frac{2}{3}\pi r^3$, multiply both sides by the reciprocal, $8 = r^3$. Apply the cube root, $r = 2$ feet, and double the radius to find the diameter of 4 feet. **See Lesson: Measurement and Dimension.**

13. C. The correct solution is 6 inches. Substitute the values into the formula, $2\pi = \frac{1}{3}\pi(1)^2 h$ and simplify using the right side of the equation by applying the exponent and multiplying, $2\pi = \frac{1}{3}\pi(1)h$, $2\pi = \frac{1}{3}\pi h$. Multiply both sides of the equation by 3 to get a solution of 6 inches. **See Lesson: Measurement and Dimension.**

14. B. The correct solution is $(-10, 10)$ because 30 can be added to the y-coordinate, $-20 + 30 = 10$. **See Lesson: Similarity, Right Triangles, and Trigonometry.**

15. D. The correct solution is 630. Substitute the values into the formula and simplify using the order of operations, $V = Bh = 63(10) = 630$ cubic inches. **See Lesson: Similarity, Right Triangles, and Trigonometry.**

16. C. The correct solution 12 units. The difference between the x-coordinates is $6-(-6) = 12$ units and the difference between the y-coordinates is $6-(-6) = 12$ units. **See Lesson: Similarity, Right Triangles, and Trigonometry.**

17. A. The first two points are on the negative x-axis, and the third point is in the first quadrant. **See Lesson: Similarity, Right Triangles, and Trigonometry.**

18. A. The correct solutions are –15.73 and –1.27. The equation can be solved by the quadratic formula.

$x = \dfrac{-17 \pm \sqrt{17^2 - 4(1)(20)}}{2(1)}$ Substitute 1 for a, 17 for b, and 20 for c.

$x = \dfrac{-17 \pm \sqrt{289 - 80}}{2}$ Apply the exponent and perform the multiplication.

$x = \dfrac{-17 \pm \sqrt{209}}{2}$ Perform the subtraction.

$x = \dfrac{-17 \pm 14.46}{2}$ Apply the square root.

$x = \dfrac{-17 + 14.46}{2}, \ x = \dfrac{-17 - 14.46}{2}$ Separate the problem into two expressions.

$x = \dfrac{-2.54}{2} = -1.27, \ x = \dfrac{-31.46}{2} = -15.73$ Simplify the numerator and divide.

See Lesson: Solving Quadratic Equations.

19. B. The correct solution is $\pm\frac{5}{2}$.

$4x^2 = 25$ Add 10 to both sides of the equation.

$x^2 = \pm\frac{25}{4}$ Divide both sides of the equation by 4.

$x = \pm\frac{5}{2}$ Apply the square root to both sides of the equation.

See Lesson: Solving Quadratic Equations.

20. D. The correct solutions are 3 and 10.

$(x–3)$ or $(x–10) = 0$ Factor the equation.

$(x–3) = 0$ or $(x–10) = 0$ Set each factor equal to 0.

$x–3 = 0$ Add 3 to both sides of the equation to solve for the first factor.

$x = 3$

$x–10 = 0$ Add 10 to both sides of the equation to solve for the second factor.

$x = 10$

See Lesson: Solving Quadratic Equations.

Made in the USA
Columbia, SC
10 April 2019